4th Workshop on Discourse in Machine Translation (DiscoMT 2019)

Hong Kong, China
3 November 2019

ISBN: 978-1-7138-0079-8

Printed from e-media with permission by:

Curran Associates, Inc.
57 Morehouse Lane
Red Hook, NY 12571

Some format issues inherent in the e-media version may also appear in this print version.

Printed with permission by Curran Associates, Inc. (2020)

Association for Computational Linguistics
209 N. Eighth Street
Stroudsburg, Pennsylvania 18360

Phone: 1-570-476-8006
Fax: 1-570-476-0860

acl@aclweb.org

Additional copies of this publication are available from:

Curran Associates, Inc.
57 Morehouse Lane
Red Hook, NY 12571 USA
Phone: 845-758-0400
Fax: 845-758-2633
Email: curran@proceedings.com
Web: www.proceedings.com

DiscoMT 2019

The Fourth Workshop on Discourse in Machine Translation

Proceedings of the Workshop

November 3, 2019
Hong Kong, China

Preface

The DiscoMT series of workshops explores the challenges and opportunities that appear when translating entire texts, as opposed to sentences in isolation. Started in 2013, the workshops are a forum for discussing novel and prospective strategies to take advantage of inter-sentential context when performing machine translation. Already a stimulating research question in the days of phrase-based statistical MT systems, the use of text-level context is both a necessity, as it enables systems to make correct translation choices, and an opportunity, as it may provide crucial information that is not available locally.

For these reasons, when translating entire texts, one cannot ignore text-level properties. This is becoming increasingly clear in neural machine translation (NMT), where text-level aspects of translation may be one of the obstacles to high-quality automatic translation for high-resource languages, after the advances in translation quality observed in recent years. Indeed, while MT of sentences removed from their contexts may seem to have reached quality levels comparable to human translations, experts still clearly prefer entire texts from human translators, as several recent evaluation studies have shown.

The first three editions of DiscoMT – held every two years – have helped to consolidate a small but thriving community of researchers. Considerable effort has been expended recently on document-level MT, such that now, several individuals and/or groups are working on similar or overlapping problems. Notable efforts include work on document-level influences on lexical choice in SMT and NMT, methods and annotated resources for discourse-level MT, discourse-sensitive assessment metrics, and specific discourse phenomena in SMT and NMT.

As exemplified by the papers presented at previous editions of DiscoMT and this year's main NLP conferences, specific research topics in document-level MT are: NMT extensions taking into consideration context from multiple sentences or entire documents; pronoun translation between languages which differ in pronoun usage; explicitation/implicitation in translating discourse connectives; context-aware translation of ambiguous terms; assessing document-level properties of MT output, including coherence; and preserving document-level properties characteristic of register, genre, and other types of text variation.

In addition to the invited talks, DiscoMT 2019 will feature oral and poster presentations of studies at the intersection of machine translation (under any of its paradigms) and discourse, from a variety of perspectives. Along with the peer-reviewed articles submitted and accepted to DiscoMT, the workshop has also invited a number of posters from EMNLP-IJCNLP, to diversify and enrich the poster session. The program thus includes a variety of MT models, especially neural ones, that consider larger contexts than state-of-the-art ones do, along with assessments of their capabilities to correctly translate discourse-level dependencies.

We hope that workshops such as this one will continue to stimulate work on Discourse and Machine Translation, in a wide range of discourse phenomena and MT architectures.

We would like to thank all the authors who submitted papers to the workshop, as well as all the members of the Program Committee who reviewed the submissions and delivered thoughtful, informative reviews.

The Chairs
October 5, 2019

Chairs

Christian Hardmeier, Uppsala University, Sweden and University of Edinburgh, UK
Sharid Loáiciga, University of Gothenburg, Sweden
Andrei Popescu-Belis, HEIG-VD/HES-SO, Switzerland
Deyi Xiong, Tianjin University, China

Program Committee:

Marine Carpuat, University of Maryland, USA
Marta Costa-jussà, Universitat Politècnica de Catalunya, Spain
Zhengxian Gong, Soochow University, Suzhou, China
Francisco Guzmán, Facebook, USA
Yulia Grishina, University of Postdam and Amazon, Berlin, Germany
Gholamreza Haffari, Monash University, Clayton, Australia
Shafiq Joty, Nanyang Technological University, Singapore
Ekaterina Lapshinova-Koltunski, Saarland University, Saarbrücken, Germany
Lesly Miculicich Werlen, Idiap Research Institute, Martigny, Switzerland
Preslav Nakov, Qatar Computing Research Institute, Doha, Qatar
Michal Novak, Charles University, Prague, Czech Republic
Nikolaos Pappas, Idiap Research Institute, Martigny, Switzerland
Lucie Poláková, Charles University, Prague, Czech Republic
Maja Popovic, Adapt Centre, Dublin City University, Ireland
Annette Rios, University of Zurich, Switzerland
Carol Scarton, University of Sheffield, UK
Rico Sennrich, University of Edinburgh, UK and University of Zurich, Switzerland
Jörg Tiedemann, University of Helsinki, Finland
Yannick Versley, Independent consultant, IBM Services, Germany
Martin Volk, University of Zurich, Switzerland
Bonnie Webber, University of Edinburgh, UK
Kellie Webster, Google, New York, USA
Min Zhang, Soochow University, Suzhou, China
Sandrine Zufferey, University of Bern, Switzerland

Table of Contents

Analysing Coreference in Transformer Outputs
Ekaterina Lapshinova-Koltunski, Cristina España-Bonet and Josef van Genabith 1

Context-Aware Neural Machine Translation Decoding
Eva Martínez Garcia, Carles Creus and Cristina España-Bonet 13

When and Why is Document-level Context Useful in Neural Machine Translation?
Yunsu Kim, Duc Thanh Tran and Hermann Ney 24

Data augmentation using back-translation for context-aware neural machine translation
Amane Sugiyama and Naoki Yoshinaga 35

Context-aware Neural Machine Translation with Coreference Information
Takumi Ohtani, Hidetaka Kamigaito, Masaaki Nagata and Manabu Okumura 45

Analysing concatenation approaches to document-level NMT in two different domains
Yves Scherrer, Jörg Tiedemann and Sharid Loáiciga 51

Conference Program

Sunday, November 3, 2019

9:00–9:05 ***Welcome***

9:05–9:50 **Session 1: Keynote Talk**

Document-level Machine Translation: the Current State and the Challenges
Professor Qun Liu, Noah's Ark Lab, Huawei

9:50–10:30 **Session 2: Poster Spotlights**

10:30–11:00 ***Coffee Break***

11:00–12:30 **Session 3: Posters**

Analysing Coreference in Transformer Outputs
Ekaterina Lapshinova-Koltunski, Cristina España-Bonet and Josef van Genabith

Context-Aware Neural Machine Translation Decoding
Eva Martínez Garcia, Carles Creus and Cristina España-Bonet

When and Why is Document-level Context Useful in Neural Machine Translation?
Yunsu Kim, Duc Thanh Tran and Hermann Ney

Data Augmentation using Back-translation for Context-aware Neural Machine Translation
Amane Sugiyama and Naoki Yoshinaga

Context-aware Neural Machine Translation with Coreference Information
Takumi Ohtani, Hidetaka Kamigaito, Masaaki Nagata and Manabu Okumura

Analysing Concatenation Approaches to Document-level NMT in two Different Domains
Yves Scherrer, Jörg Tiedemann and Sharid Loáiciga

Additional invited posters from the main conference

Analysing Coreference in Transformer Outputs

Ekaterina Lapshinova-Koltunski
Saarland University

Cristina España-Bonet
Saarland University
DFKI GmbH

Josef van Genabith
Saarland University
DFKI GmbH

e.lapshinova@mx.uni-saarland.de
{cristinae,Josef.Van_Genabith}@dfki.de

Abstract

We analyse coreference phenomena in three neural machine translation systems trained with different data settings with or without access to explicit intra- and cross-sentential anaphoric information. We compare system performance on two different genres: news and TED talks. To do this, we manually annotate (the possibly incorrect) coreference chains in the MT outputs and evaluate the coreference chain translations. We define an error typology that aims to go further than pronoun translation adequacy and includes types such as incorrect word selection or missing words. The features of coreference chains in automatic translations are also compared to those of the source texts and human translations. The analysis shows stronger potential translationese effects in machine translated outputs than in human translations.

1 Introduction

In the present paper, we analyse coreference in the output of three neural machine translation systems (NMT) that were trained under different settings. We use a transformer architecture (Vaswani et al., 2017) and train it on corpora of different sizes with and without the specific coreference information. Transformers are the current state-of-the-art in NMT (Barrault et al., 2019) and are solely based on attention, therefore, the kind of errors they produce might be different from other architectures such as CNN or RNN-based ones. Here we focus on one architecture to study the different errors produced only under different data configurations.

Coreference is an important component of discourse coherence which is achieved in how discourse entities (and events) are introduced and discussed. Coreference chains contain mentions of one and the same discourse element throughout a text. These mentions are realised by a variety of linguistic devices such as pronouns, nominal phrases (NPs) and other linguistic means. As languages differ in the range of such linguistic means (Lapshinova-Koltunski et al., 2019; Kunz and Lapshinova-Koltunski, 2015; Novák and Nedoluzhko, 2015; Kunz and Steiner, 2012) and in their contextual restrictions (Kunz et al., 2017), these differences give rise to problems that may result in incoherent (automatic) translations. We focus on coreference chains in English-German translations belonging to two different genres. In German, pronouns, articles and adjectives (and some nouns) are subject to grammatical gender agreement, whereas in English, only person pronouns carry gender marking. An incorrect translation of a pronoun or a nominal phrase may lead to an incorrect relation in a discourse and will destroy a coreference chain.

Recent studies in automatic coreference translation have shown that dedicated systems can lead to improvements in pronoun translation (Guillou et al., 2016; Loáiciga et al., 2017). However, standard NMT systems work at sentence level, so improvements in NMT translate into improvements on pronouns with intra-sentential antecedents, but the phenomenon of coreference is not limited to anaphoric pronouns, and even less to a subset of them. Document-level machine translation (MT) systems are needed to deal with coreference as a whole. Although some attempts to include extra-sentential information exist (Wang et al., 2017; Voita et al., 2018; Jean and Cho, 2019; Junczys-Dowmunt, 2019), the problem is far from being solved. Besides that, some further problems of NMT that do not seem to be related to coreference at first glance (such as translation of unknown words and proper names or the hallucination of additional words) cause coreference-related errors.

In our work, we focus on the analysis of complete coreference chains, manually annotating

Proceedings of the Fourth Workshop on Discourse in Machine Translation (DiscoMT 2019), pages 1–12
Hong Kong, China, November 3, 2019. ©2019 Association for Computational Linguistics

them in the three translation variants. We also evaluate them from the point of view of coreference chain translation. The goal of this paper is two-fold. On the one hand, we are interested in various properties of coreference chains in these translations. They include total number of chains, average chain length, the size of the longest chain and the total number of annotated mentions. These features are compared to those of the underlying source texts and also the corresponding human translation reference. On the other hand, we are also interested in the quality of coreference translations. Therefore, we define a typology of errors, and and chain members in MT output are annotated as to whether or not they are correct. The main focus is on such errors as gender, number and case of the mentions, but we also consider wrong word selection or missing words in a chain. Unlike previous work, we do not restrict ourselves to pronouns. Our analyses show that there are further errors that are not directly related to coreference but consequently have an influence on the correctness of coreference chains.

The remainder of the paper is organised as follows. Section 2 introduces the main concepts and presents an overview of related MT studies. Section 3 provides details on the data, systems used and annotation procedures. Section 4 analyses the performance of our transformer systems on coreferent mentions. Finally we summarise and draw conclusions in Section 5.

2 Background and Related Work

2.1 Coreference

Coreference is related to cohesion and coherence. The latter is the logical flow of inter-related ideas in a text, whereas cohesion refers to the text-internal relationship of linguistic elements that are overtly connected via lexico-grammatical devices across sentences (Halliday and Hasan, 1976). As stated by Hardmeier (2012, p. 3), this connectedness of texts implies dependencies between sentences. And if these dependencies are neglected in translation, the output text no longer has the property of connectedness which makes a sequence of sentences a text. Coreference expresses identity to a referent mentioned in another textual part (not necessarily in neighbouring sentences) contributing to text connectedness. An addressee is following the mentioned referents and identifies them when they are repeated. Identification of certain referents depends not only on a lexical form, but also on other linguistic means, e.g. articles or modifying pronouns (Kibrik, 2011). The use of these is influenced by various factors which can be language-dependent (range of linguistic means available in grammar) and also context-independent (pragmatic situation, genre). Thus, the means of expressing reference differ across languages and genres. This has been shown by some studies in the area of contrastive linguistics (Kunz et al., 2017; Kunz and Lapshinova-Koltunski, 2015; Kunz and Steiner, 2012). Analyses in cross-lingual coreference resolution (Grishina, 2017; Grishina and Stede, 2015; Novák and Žabokrtský, 2014; Green et al., 2011) show that there are still unsolved problems that should be addressed.

2.2 Translation studies

Differences between languages and genres in the linguistic means expressing reference are important for translation, as the choice of an appropriate referring expression in the target language poses challenges for both human and machine translation. In translation studies, there is a number of corpus-based works analysing these differences in translation. However, most of them are restricted to individual phenomena within coreference. For instance, Zinsmeister et al. (2012) analyse abstract anaphors in English-German translations. To our knowledge, they do not consider chains. Lapshinova-Koltunski and Hardmeier (2017b) in their contrastive analysis of potential coreference chain members in English-German translations, describe transformation patterns that contain different types of referring expressions. However, the authors rely on automatic tagging and parsing procedures and do not include chains into their analysis. The data used by Novák and Nedoluzhko (2015) and Novák (2018) contain manual chain annotations. The authors focus on different categories of anaphoric pronouns in English-Czech translations, though not paying attention to chain features (e.g. their number or size).

Chain features are considered in a contrastive analysis by Kunz et al. (2017). Their study concerns different phenomena in a variety of genres in English and German comparable texts. Using contrastive interpretations, they suggest preferred translation strategies from English into German, i.e. translators should use demonstrative pronouns instead of personal pronouns (e.g. *dies/das* instead of *es/it*) when translating from English into German and vice versa. However, corpus-based studies show that translators do not necessarily apply such strategies. Instead, they often preserve the source language anaphor's categories (as shown e.g. by Zinsmeister et al., 2012) which results in the shining through effects (Teich, 2003). Moreover, due to the tendency of translators to explicitly realise meanings in translations that were implicit in the source texts (explicitation effects, Blum-Kulka, 1986), translations are believed to contain more (explicit) referring expressions, and subsequently, more (and longer) coreference chains.

Therefore, in our analysis, we focus on the chain features related to the phenomena of shining through and explicitation. These features include number of mentions, number of chains, average chain length and the longest chain size. Machine-translated texts are compared to their sources and the corresponding human translations in terms of these features. We expect to find shining through and explicitation effects in automatic translations.

2.3 Coreference in MT

As explained in the introduction, several recent works tackle the automatic translation of pronouns and also coreference (for instance, Voigt and Jurafsky, 2012; Miculicich Werlen and Popescu-Belis, 2017) and this has, in part, motivated the creation of devoted shared tasks and test sets to evaluate the quality of pronoun translation (Guillou et al., 2016; Webber et al., 2017; Guillou et al., 2018; Bawden et al., 2018).

But coreference is a wider phenomenon that affects more linguistic elements. Noun phrases also appear in coreference chains but they are usually studied under coherence and consistency in MT. Xiong et al. (2015) use topic modelling to extract coherence chains in the source, predict them in the target and then promote them as translations. Martínez et al. (2017) use word embeddings to enforce consistency within documents. Before these works, several methods to post-process the translations and even including a second decoding pass were used (Carpuat, 2009; Xiao et al., 2011; Ture et al., 2012; Martínez et al., 2014).

Recent NMT systems that include context deal with both phenomena, coreference and coherence, but usually context is limited to the previous sentence, so chains as a whole are never considered. Voita et al. (2018) encode both a source and a context sentence and then combine them to obtain a context-aware input. The same idea was implemented before by Tiedemann and Scherrer (2017) where they concatenate a source sentence with the previous one to include context. Caches (Tu et al., 2018), memory networks (Maruf and Haffari, 2018) and hierarchical attention methods (Miculicich et al., 2018) allow to use a wider context. Finally, our work is also related to Stojanovski and Fraser (2018) and Stojanovski and Fraser (2019) where their oracle translations are similar to the data-based approach we introduce in Section 3.1.

	# lines	S1, S3	S2
Common Crawl	2,394,878	x1	x4
Europarl	1,775,445	x1	x4
News Commentary	328,059	x4	x16
Rapid	1,105,651	x1	x4
ParaCrawl Filtered	12,424,790	x0	x1

Table 1: Number of lines of the corpora used for training the NMT systems under study. The 2nd and 3rd columns show the amount of oversampling used.

3 Systems, Methods and Resources

3.1 State-of-the-art NMT

Our NMT systems are based on a transformer architecture (Vaswani et al., 2017) as implemented in the `Marian` toolkit (Junczys-Dowmunt et al., 2018) using the *transformer big* configuration.

We train three systems (S1, S2 and S3) with the corpora summarised in Table 1.[1] The first two systems are transformer models trained on different amounts of data (6M vs. 18M parallel sentences as seen in the Table). The third system includes a modification to consider the information of full coreference chains throughout a document augmenting the sentence to be translated with this information and it is trained with the same amount of sentence pairs as S1. A variant of the S3 system participated in the news machine translation of the shared task held at WMT 2019 (España-Bonet et al., 2019).

S1 is trained with the concatenation of Common Crawl, Europarl, a cleaned version of Rapid and

[1] All corpora are freely available for the WMT news translation task and can be downloaded from `http://www.statmt.org/wmt19/translation-task.html`

the News Commentary corpus. We oversample the latter in order to have a significant representation of data close to the news genre in the final corpus.

S2 uses the same data as S1 with the addition of a filtered portion of Paracrawl. This corpus is known to be noisy, so we use it to create a larger training corpus but it is diluted by a factor 4 to give more importance to high quality translations.

S3 S3 uses the same data as S1, but this time enriched with the cross- and intra-sentential coreference chain markup as described below.[2] The information is included as follows.

Source documents are annotated with coreference chains using the neural annotator of `Stanford CoreNLP` (Manning et al., 2014)[3]. The tool detects pronouns, nominal phrases and proper names as mentions in a chain. For every mention, `CoreNLP` extracts its gender (male, female, neutral, unknown), number (singular, plural, unknown), and animacy (animate, inanimate, unknown). This information is not added directly but used to enrich the single sentence-based MT training data by applying a set of heuristics implemented in `DocTrans`[4]:

1. We enrich *pronominal mentions* with the exception of "I" with the head (main noun phrase) of the chain. The head is cleaned by removing articles and Saxon genitives and we only consider heads with less than 4 tokens in order to avoid enriching a word with a full sentence
2. We enrich *nominal mentions* including *proper names* with the gender of the head
3. The head itself is enriched with she/he/it/they depending on its gender and animacy

The enrichment is done with the addition of tags as shown in the examples:

- I never cook with *<b_crf> salt <e_crf>* it.
- *<b_crf> she <e_crf>* Biles arrived late.

In the first case heuristic 1 is used, *salt* is the head of the chain and it is prepended to the pronoun. The second example shows a sentence where heuristic 2 has been used and the proper name *Biles* has now information about the gender of the person it is referring to.

Afterwards, the NMT system is trained at sentence level in the usual way. The data used for the three systems is cleaned, tokenised, truecased with Moses scripts[5] and BPEd with subword-nmt[6] using separated vocabularies with 50 k subword units each. The validation set ($news2014$) and the test sets described in the following section are preprocessed in the same way.

3.2 Test data under analysis

As one of our aims is to compare coreference chain properties in automatic translation with those of the source texts and human reference, we derive data from ParCorFull, an English-German corpus annotated with full coreference chains (Lapshinova-Koltunski et al., 2018).[7] The corpus contains ca. 160.7 thousand tokens manually annotated with about 14.9 thousand mentions and 4.7 thousand coreference chains. For our analysis, we select a portion of English news texts and TED talks from ParCorFull and translate them with the three NMT systems described in 3.1 above. As texts considerably differ in their length, we select 17 news texts (494 sentences) and four TED talks (518 sentences). The size (in tokens) of the total data set under analysis – source (src) and human translations (ref) from ParCorFull and the automatic translations produced within this study (S1, S2 and S3) are presented in Table 2.

Notably, automatic translations of TED talks contain more words than the corresponding reference translation, which means that machine-translated texts of this type have also more potential tokens to enter in a coreference relation, and potentially indicating a shining through effect. The same does not happen with the news test set.

3.3 Manual annotation process

The English sources and their corresponding human translations into German were already manually annotated for coreference chains. We follow the same scheme as Lapshinova-Koltunski and Hardmeier (2017a) to annotate the MT outputs with coreference chains. This scheme allows

[2]Paracrawl has document boundaries but with a mean of 1.06 sent/doc which makes it useless within our approach.

[3]This system achieves a precision of 80% and recall of 70% on the CoNLL 2012 English Test Data (Clark and Manning, 2016). Voita et al. (2018) estimated an accuracy of 79% on the translation of the pronoun *it*.

[4]`https://github.com/cristinae/DocTrans/`

[5]`https://github.com/moses-smt/mosesdecoder/tree/master/scripts`

[6]`https://github.com/rsennrich/subword-nmt`

[7]Available at `https://lindat.mff.cuni.cz/repository/xmlui/handle/11372/LRT-2614`

	news					TED				
	tokens	#ment.	#chains	avg. length	max. length	tokens	# ment.	#chains	avg. length	max. length
src	9,862	782	176	5.1	15.8	11,155	1,042	338	2.9	34.7
src$_{\text{CoreNLP}}$	10,502	915	385	2.3	13.2	11,753	989	407	2.4	30.3
ref	9,728	851	233	3.8	14.5	10,140	916	318	2.8	38.0
S1	9,613	1,216	302	4.2	17.2	10,547	1,270	293	4.5	47.0
S2	9,609	1,218	302	4.4	17.3	10,599	1,268	283	4.6	51.7
S3	9,589	1,174	290	4.3	16.2	10,305	1,277	280	4.7	47.0

Table 2: Statistics on coreference features for news and TED texts considered.

the annotator to define each markable as a certain mention type (pronoun, NP, VP or clause). The mentions can be defined further in terms of their cohesive function (antecedent, anaphoric, cataphoric, comparative, substitution, ellipsis, apposition). Antecedents can either be marked as simple or split or as entity or event. The annotation scheme also includes pronoun type (personal, possessive, demonstrative, reflexive, relative) and modifier types of NPs (possessive, demonstrative, definite article, or none for proper names), see (Lapshinova-Koltunski et al., 2018) for details. The mentions referring to the same discourse item are linked between each other. We use the annotation tool MMAX2 (Müller and Strube, 2006) which was also used for the annotation of ParCorFull.

In the next step, chain members are annotated for their correctness. For the incorrect translations of mentions, we include the following error categories: *gender*, *number*, *case*, *ambiguous* and *other*. The latter category is open, which means that the annotators can add their own error types during the annotation process. With this, the final typology of errors also considered *wrong named entity*, *wrong word*, *missing word*, *wrong syntactic structure*, *spelling error* and *addressee reference*.

The annotation of machine-translated texts was integrated into a university course on discourse phenomena. Our annotators, well-trained students of linguistics, worked in small groups on the assigned annotation tasks (4-5 texts, i.e. 12-15 translations per group). At the beginning of the annotation process, the categories under analysis were discussed within the small groups and also in the class. The final versions of the annotation were then corrected by the instructor.

4 Results and Analyses

4.1 Chain features

First, we compare the distribution of several chain features in the three MT outputs, their source texts and the corresponding human translations.

Table 2 shows that, overall, all machine translations contain a greater number of annotated mentions in both news texts and TED talks than in the annotated source (*src* and *src*$_{\text{CoreNLP}}$) and reference (*ref*) texts. Notice that src$_{\text{CoreNLP}}$ —where coreferences are not manually but automatically annotated with `CoreNLP`— counts also the tokens that the mentions add to the sentences, but not the tags. The larger number of mentions may indicate a strong explicitation effect observed in machine-translated texts. Interestingly, `CoreNLP` detects a similar number of mentions in both genres, while human annotators clearly marked more chains for TED than for news. Both genres are in fact quite different in nature; whereas only 37% of the mentions are pronominal in news texts (343 out of 915), the number grows to 58% for TED (577 out of 989), and this could be an indicator of the difficulty of the genres for NMT systems.

There is also a variation in terms of chain number between translations of TED talks and news. While automatic translations of news texts contain more chains than the corresponding human annotated sources and references, machine-translated TED talks contain less chains than the sources and human translations. However, there is not much variation between the chain features of the three MT outputs. The chains are also longer in machine-translated output than in reference translations as can be seen by the number of mentions per chain and the length of the longest chain.

	news$_{all}$		news$_{coref}$			TED$_{all}$		TED$_{coref}$		
	BLEU	MTR	BLEU	MTR	#mention err.	BLEU	MTR	BLEU	MTR	#mention err.
S1	30.68	55.87	30.07	55.84	117 (9.6%)	31.99	57.91	31.70	58.06	84 (6.6%)
S2	31.47	56.88	30.83	56.68	86 (7.1%)	32.36	58.22	32.81	59.73	105 (8.3%)
S3	30.35	55.26	29.89	55.24	121 (10.3%)	32.67	58.84	32.84	58.85	83 (6.5%)

Table 3: BLEU and METEOR (MTR) scores for the 3 systems on our full test set (all) and the subset of sentences where coreference occurrs ($coref$). The number of erroneous mentions is shown for comparison.

4.2 MT quality at system level

We evaluate the quality of the three transformer engines with two automatic metrics, BLEU (Papineni et al., 2002) and METEOR (Banerjee and Lavie, 2005). Table 3 shows the scores in two cases: *all*, when the complete texts are evaluated and *coref*, when only the subset of sentences that have been augmented in S3 are considered – 265 out of 494 for news and 239 out of 518 for TED. For news, the best system is that trained on more data, S2; but for TED talks S3 with less data has the best performance.

The difference between the behaviour of the systems can be related to the different genres. We have seen that news are dominated by nominal mentions while TED is dominated by pronominal ones. Pronouns mostly need coreference information to be properly translated, while noun phrases can be improved simply because more instances of the nouns appear in the training data. With this, S3 improves the baseline S1 in +1.1 BLEU points for TED$_{coref}$ but -0.2 BLEU points for news$_{coref}$.

However, even if the systems differ in the overall performance, the change is not related to the number of errors in coreference chains. Table 3 also reports the number of mistakes in the translation of coreferent mentions. Whereas the number of errors correlates with translation quality (as measured by BLEU) for news$_{coref}$ this is not the case of TED$_{coref}$.

4.3 Error analysis

The total distribution for the 10 categories of errors defined in Section 3.3 can be seen in Figure 1. Globally, the proportion of errors due to our closed categories (gender, number, case and ambiguous) is larger for TED talks than for news (see analysis in Section 4.3.1). Gender is an issue with all systems and genres which does not get solved by the addition of more data. Additionally, news struggle with wrong words and named entities; for this genre the additional error types (see analysis in Section 4.3.2) represent around 60% of the errors of S1/S3 to be compared to the 40% of TED talks.

4.3.1 Predefined error categories

Within our predefined closed categories (gender, number, case and ambiguous), the gender errors belong to the most frequent errors. They include wrong gender translation of both pronouns, as *sie* ("her") instead of *ihn* ("him") in example (1) referring to the masculine noun *Mindestlohn*, and nominal phrases, as *der Stasi* instead of *die Stasi*, where a masculine form of the definite article is used instead of a feminine one, in example (2).

(1) src: *[The current minimum wage] of 7.25 US dollars is a pittance... She wants to raise [it] to 15 dollars an hour.*
S3: *[Der aktuelle Mindestlohn] von 7,25 US-Dollar sei Almosen... Sie möchte [sie] auf 15 Dollar pro Stunde erhhen.*

(2) src: *...let's have a short look at the history of [the Stasi], because it is really important for understanding [its] self-conception.*
S2: *Lassen sie uns... einen kurzen Blick auf die Geschichte [des Stasi] werfen denn es wirklich wichtig, [seine] Selbstauffassung zu verstehen.*

The gender-related errors are common to all the automatic translations. Interestingly, systems S1 and S3 have more problems with gender in translations of TED talks, whereas they do better in translating news, which leads us to assume that this is a data-dependent issue: while the antecedent for news is in the same sentence it is not for TED talks. A closer look at the texts with a high number of gender problems confirms this assumption —they contain references to females who were translated with male forms of nouns and pronouns (e.g. *Mannschaftskapitän* instead of *Mannschaftskapitänin*).

We also observe errors related to gender for the cases of explicitation in translation. Some impersonal English constructions not having direct equivalents in German are translated with personal constructions, which requires an addition of a pronoun. Such cases of explicitation were automatically detected in parallel data in (Lapshinova-Koltunski and Hardmeier, 2017b; Lapshinova-Koltunski et al., 2019). They belong to the category of obligatory explicitation, i.e. explicitation dictated by differences in the syntactic and semantic structure of languages, as defined by Klaudy (2008). An MT system tends to insert a male form instead of a female one even if it's marked as feminine (S3 adds the feminine form *she* as markup), as illustrated in example (3) where the automatic translation contains the masculine pronoun *er* ("he") instead of *sie* ("she").

(3) src: *[Biles] earned the first one on Tuesday while serving as the exclamation point to retiring national team coordinator Martha Karolyi's going away party.*
ref: *[Biles] holte die erste Medaille am Dienstag, während [sie] auf der Abschiedsfeier der sich in Ruhestand begehenden Mannschaftskoordinatorin Martha Karolyi als Ausrufezeichen diente.*
S2: *[Biles] verdiente den ersten am Dienstag, während [er] als Ausrufezeichen für den pensionierten Koordinator der Nationalmannschaft, Martha Karolyi, diente.*

Another interesting case of a problem related to gender is the dependence of the referring expressions on grammatical restrictions in German. In example (4), the source chain contains the pronoun *him* referring to both *a 6-year-old boy* and *The child*. In German, these two nominal phrases have different gender (masculine vs. neutral). The pronoun has grammatical agreement with the second noun of the chain (*des Kindes*) and not its head (*ein 6 Jahre alter Junge*).

(4) src: *Police say [a 6-year-old boy] has been shot in Philadelphia... [The child]'s grandparents identified [him] to CBS Philadelphia as [Mahaj Brown].*
S1: *Die Polizei behauptet, [ein 6 Jahre alter Junge] sei in Philadelphia erschossen worden... Die Großeltern [des Kindes] identifizierten [ihn] mit CBS Philadelphia als [Mahaj Brown].*

Case- and number-related errors are less frequent in our data. However, translations of TED talks with S2 contain much more number-related errors than other outputs. Example (5) illustrates this error type which occurs within a sentence. The English source contains the nominal chain in singular *the cost – it*, whereas the German correspondence *Kosten* has a plural form and requires a plural pronoun (*sie*). However, the automatic translation contains the singular pronoun *es*.

(5) src: *...to the point where [the cost] is now below 1,000 dollars, and it's confidently predicted that by the year 2015 [it] will be below 100 dollars...*
S2: *bis zu dem Punkt, wo [die Kosten] jetzt unter 1.000 Dollar liegen, und es ist zuversichtlich, dass [es] bis zum Jahr 2015 unter 100 Dollar liegen wird...*

Ambiguous cases often contain a combination of errors or they are difficult to categorise due to the ambiguity of the source pronouns, as the pronoun *it* in example (6) which may refer either to the noun *trouble* or even the clause *Democracy is in trouble* is translated with the pronoun *sie* (feminine). In case of the first meaning, the pronoun would be correct, but the form of the following verb should be in plural. In case of a singular form, we would need to use a demonstrative pronoun *dies* (or possibly the personal pronoun *es*).

(6) src: *Democracy is in trouble... and [it] comes in part from a deep dilemma...*
S2: *Die Demokratie steckt in Schwierigkeiten ... und [sie] rührt teilweise aus einem tiefen Dilemma her...*

4.3.2 Additional error types

At first glance, the error types discussed in this section do not seem to be related to coreference — a wrong translation of a noun can be traced back to the training data available and the way NMT deals with unknown words. However, a wrong translation of a noun may result in its invalidity to be a referring expression for a certain discourse item. As a consequence, a coreference chain is damaged. We illustrate a chain with a wrong named entity translation in example (7). The source chain contains five nominal mentions referring to an American gymnast Aly Raisman: *silver medalist* – "Final Five" teammate – *Aly Raisman* – *Aly Raisman* – *Raisman*. All the three systems used different names. Example (7) illustrates the trans-

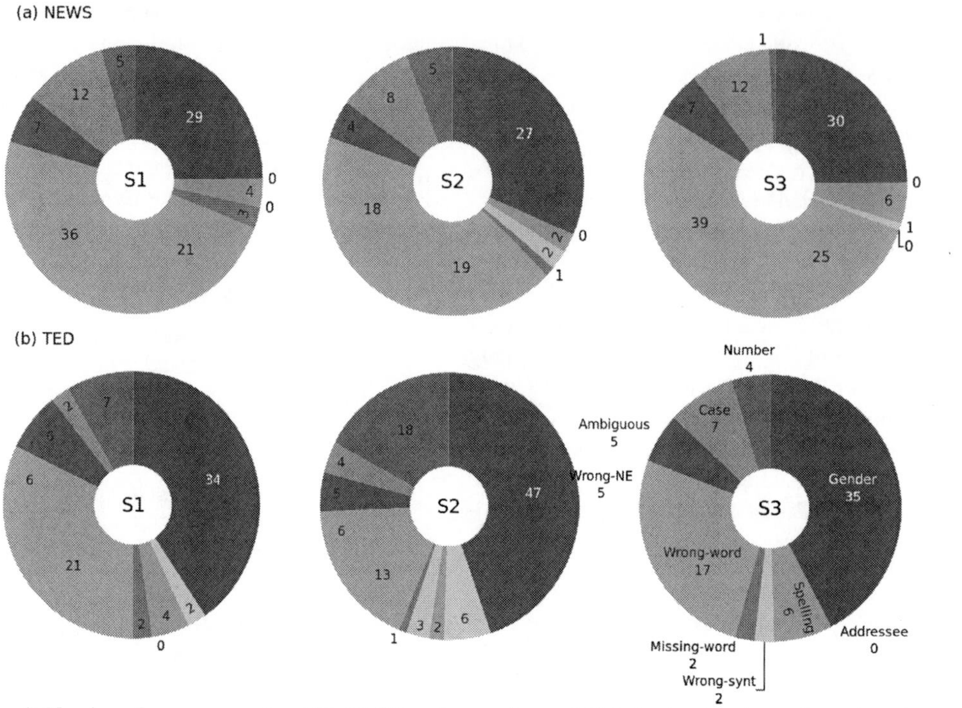

Figure 1: Number of errors per system (S1, S2, S3) and genre (news, TED). Notice that the total number of errors differs for each plot, total numbers are reported in Table 3. Labels in Figure (b)–S3 apply to all the chart pies that use the same order and color scale for the different error types defined in Section 4.3.

lation with S2, where *Aly Donovan* and *Aly Encence* were used instead of *Aly Raisman*, and the mention *Raisman* disappears completely from the chain.

(7) src: *Her total of 62.198 was well clear of [silver medalist] and ["Final Five" teammate] [Aly Raisman]...United States' Simone Biles, left, and [Aly Raisman] embrace after winning gold and silver respectively... [Raisman]'s performance was a bit of revenge from four years ago, when [she] tied...*
S2: *Ihre Gesamtmenge von 62.198 war deutlich von [Silbermedaillengewinner] und ["Final Five" Teamkollegen] [Aly Donovan]... Die Vereinigten Staaten Simone Biles, links und [Aly Encence] Umarmung nach dem Gewinn von Gold und Silber... Vor vier Jahren, als [sie]...*

Example (8) illustrates translation of the chain *The scaling in the opposite direction – that scale.* The noun phrases *Die Verlagerung in die entgegengesetzte Richtung* ("the shift in the opposite direction") and *dieses Ausmaß* ("extent/scale") used in the S1 output do not corefer (cf. *Wachstum in die entgegengesetzte Richtung* and *Wachstum* in the reference translation). Notice that these cases with long noun phrases are not tackled by S3 either.

(8) src: *[The scaling in the opposite direction]...drive the structure of business towards the creation of new kinds of institutions that can achieve [that scale].*
ref: *[Wachstum in die entgegengesetzte Richtung]... steuert die Struktur der Geschäfte in Richtung Erschaffung von neuen Institutionen, die [dieses Wachstum] erreichen können.*
S1: *[Die Verlagerung in die entgegengesetzte Richtung]... treibt die Struktur der Unternehmen in Richtung der Schaffung neuer Arten von Institutionen, die [dieses Ausmaß] erreichen können.*

4.3.3 Types of erroneous mentions

Finally, we also analyse the types of the mentions marked as errors. They include either nominal phrases or pronouns. Table 4 shows that there is a variation between the news texts and TED talks

		ant.	ana.	NP	pron.
news	**S1**	0.30	0.70	0.72	0.28
news	**S2**	0.39	0.61	0.63	0.37
news	**S3**	0.36	0.64	0.63	0.37
TED	**S1**	0.18	0.82	0.36	0.64
TED	**S2**	0.18	0.82	0.34	0.66
TED	**S3**	0.28	0.72	0.46	0.54

Table 4: Percentage of erroneous mentions: antecedent vs. anaphor, and noun phrase vs. pronominal.

in terms of these features. News contain more erroneous nominal phrases, whereas TED talks contain more pronoun-related errors. Whereas both the news and the TED talks have more errors in translating anaphors, there is a higher proportion of erroneous antecedents in the news than in the TED talks.

It is also interesting to see that S3 reduces the percentage of errors in anaphors for TED, but has a similar performance to S2 on news.

5 Summary and Conclusions

We analysed coreferences in the translation outputs of three transformer systems that differ in the training data and in whether they have access to explicit intra- and cross-sentential anaphoric information (S3) or not (S1, S2). We see that the translation errors are more dependent on the genre than on the nature of the specific NMT system: whereas news (with mainly NP mentions) contain a majority of errors related to wrong word selection, TED talks (with mainly pronominal mentions) are prone to accumulate errors on gender and number.

System S3 was specifically designed to solve this issue, but we cannot trace the improvement from S1 to S3 by just counting the errors and error types, as some errors disappear and others emerge: coreference quality and automatic translation quality do not correlate in our analysis on TED talks. As a further improvement to address the issue, we could add more parallel data to our training corpus with a higher density of coreference chains such as movie subtitles or parallel TED talks.

We also characterised the originals and translations according to coreference features such as total number of chains and mentions, average chain length and size of the longest chain. We see how NMT translations increase the number of mentions about 30% with respect to human references showing even a more marked explicitation effect than human translations do. As future work, we consider a more detailed comparison of the human and machine translations, and analyse the purpose of the additional mentions added by the NMT systems. It would be also interesting to evaluate of the quality of the automatically computed coreferences chains used for S3.

Acknowledgments

The annotation work was performed at Saarland University. We thank Anna Felsing, Francesco Fernicola, Viktoria Henn, Johanna Irsch, Kira Janine Jebing, Alicia Lauer, Friederike Lessau and Christina Pollkläsener for performing the manual annotation of the NMT outputs. The project on which this paper is based was partially funded by the German Federal Ministry of Education and Research under the funding code 01IW17001 (Deeplee) and by the German Research Foundation (DFG) as part of SFB 1102 Information Density and Linguistic Encoding. Responsibility for the content of this publication is with the authors.

References

Satanjeev Banerjee and Alon Lavie. 2005. METEOR: An Automatic Metric for MT Evaluation with Improved Correlation with Human Judgments. In *Proceedings of Workshop on Intrinsic and Extrinsic Evaluation Measures for MT and/or Summarization at the 43rd Annual Meeting of the Association of Computational Linguistics (ACL-2005)*, Ann Arbor, Michigan.

Loïc Barrault, Ondřej Bojar, Marta R. Costa-jussà, Christian Federmann, Mark Fishel, Yvette Graham, Barry Haddow, Matthias Huck, Philipp Koehn, Shervin Malmasi, Christof Monz, Mathias Mller, Santanu Pal, Matt Post, and Marcos Zampieri. 2019. Findings of the 2019 Conference on Machine Translation (WMT19). In *Proceedings of the Fourth Conference on Machine Translation (Volume 2: Shared Task Papers, Day 1)*, pages 1–61, Florence, Italy. Association for Computational Linguistics.

Rachel Bawden, Rico Sennrich, Alexandra Birch, and Barry Haddow. 2018. Evaluating Discourse Phenomena in Neural Machine Translation. In *Proceedings of the 2018 Conference of the North American Chapter of the Association for Computational Linguistics: Human Language Technologies, Volume 1 (Long Papers)*, pages 1304–1313, New Orleans, Louisiana. Association for Computational Linguistics.

Shoshana Blum-Kulka. 1986. Shifts of cohesion and coherence in translation. In Juliane House and

Shoshana Blum-Kulka, editors, *Interlingual and intercultural communication*, pages 17–35. Gunter Narr, Tübingen.

Marine Carpuat. 2009. One Translation Per Discourse. In *Proceedings of the Workshop on Semantic Evaluations: Recent Achievements and Future Directions (SEW)*, pages 19–27.

Kevin Clark and Christopher D. Manning. 2016. Deep Reinforcement Learning for Mention-Ranking Coreference Models. In *Proceedings of the 2016 Conference on Empirical Methods in Natural Language Processing*, pages 2256–2262, Austin, Texas. Association for Computational Linguistics.

Cristina España-Bonet, Dana Ruiter, and Josef van Genabith. 2019. UdS-DFKI Participation at WMT 2019: Low-Resource (*en–gu*) and Coreference-Aware (*en–de*) Systems. In *Proceedings of the Fourth Conference on Machine Translation*, pages 382–389, Florence, Italy. Association for Computational Linguistics.

Spence Green, Nicholas Andrews, Matthew R Gormley, Mark Dredze, and Christopher D Manning. 2011. Cross-lingual coreference resolution: A new task for multilingual comparable corpora. Technical Report 6, HLTCOE, Johns Hopkins University.

Yulia Grishina. 2017. Combining the output of two coreference resolution systems for two source languages to improve annotation projection. In *Proceedings of the Third Workshop on Discourse in Machine Translation (DiscoMT), EMNLP 2017*, Copenhagen, Denmark.

Yulia Grishina and Manfred Stede. 2015. Knowledge-lean projection of coreference chains across languages. In *Proceedings of the 8th Workshop on Building and Using Comparable Corpora*, page 14, Beijing, China.

Liane Guillou, Christian Hardmeier, Ekaterina Lapshinova-Koltunski, and Sharid Loáiciga. 2018. A Pronoun Test Suite Evaluation of the English-German MT Systems at WMT 2018. In *Proceedings of the Third Conference on Machine Translation: Shared Task Papers, WMT 2018, Belgium, Brussels, October 31 - November 1, 2018*, pages 570–577.

Liane Guillou, Christian Hardmeier, Preslav Nakov, Sara Stymne, Jörg Tiedemann, Yannick Versley, Mauro Cettolo, Bonnie Webber, and Andrei Popescu-Belis. 2016. Findings of the 2016 WMT Shared Task on Cross-lingual Pronoun Prediction. In *Proceedings of the First Conference on Machine Translation: Volume 2, Shared Task Papers*, pages 525–542, Berlin, Germany. Association for Computational Linguistics.

M.A.K. Halliday and Ruqaiya Hasan. 1976. *Cohesion in English*. Longman, London, New York.

Christian Hardmeier. 2012. Discourse in Statistical Machine Translation: A Survey and a Case Study. *Discours – Revue de linguistique, psycholinguistique et informatique*, 11.

Sébastien Jean and Kyunghyun Cho. 2019. Context-Aware Learning for Neural Machine Translation. *CoRR*, abs/1903.04715.

Marcin Junczys-Dowmunt. 2019. Microsoft Translator at WMT 2019: Towards Large-Scale Document-Level Neural Machine Translation. In *Proceedings of the Fourth Conference on Machine Translation (Volume 2: Shared Task Papers, Day 1)*, pages 225–233, Florence, Italy. Association for Computational Linguistics.

Marcin Junczys-Dowmunt, Roman Grundkiewicz, Tomasz Dwojak, Hieu Hoang, Kenneth Heafield, Tom Neckermann, Frank Seide, Ulrich Germann, Alham Fikri Aji, Nikolay Bogoychev, André F. T. Martins, and Alexandra Birch. 2018. Marian: Fast Neural Machine Translation in C++. In *Proceedings of ACL 2018, System Demonstrations*, pages 116–121, Melbourne, Australia. Association for Computational Linguistics.

Andrej A. Kibrik. 2011. *Reference in discourse*. Oxford University Press, Oxford.

Kinga Klaudy. 2008. Explicitation. In M. Baker and G. Saldanha, editors, *Routledge Encyclopedia of Translation Studies*, 2 edition, pages 104–108. Routledge, London & New York.

Kerstin Kunz, Stefania Degaetano-Ortlieb, Ekaterina Lapshinova-Koltunski, Katrin Menzel, and Erich Steiner. 2017. GECCo – an empirically-based comparison of English-German cohesion. In Gert De Sutter, Marie-Aude Lefer, and Isabelle Delaere, editors, *Empirical Translation Studies: New Methodological and Theoretical Traditions*, volume 300 of *TILSM series*, pages 265–312. Mouton de Gruyter. TILSM series.

Kerstin Kunz and Ekaterina Lapshinova-Koltunski. 2015. Cross-linguistic analysis of discourse variation across registers. *Special Issue of Nordic Journal of English Studies*, 14(1):258–288.

Kerstin Kunz and Erich Steiner. 2012. Towards a comparison of cohesive reference in English and German: System and text. In M. Taboada, S. Doval Surez, and E. Gonzlez lvarez, editors, *Contrastive Discourse Analysis. Functional and Corpus Perspectives*. Equinox, London.

Ekaterina Lapshinova-Koltunski and Christian Hardmeier. 2017a. *Coreference Corpus Annotation Guidelines*.

Ekaterina Lapshinova-Koltunski and Christian Hardmeier. 2017b. Discovery of Discourse-Related Language Contrasts through Alignment Discrepancies in English-German Translation. In *Proceedings of the Third Workshop on Discourse in Machine Translation (DiscoMT 2017) at EMNLP-2017*, Copenhagen, Denmark.

Ekaterina Lapshinova-Koltunski, Christian Hardmeier, and Marie-Pauline Krielke. 2018. ParCorFull: a Parallel Corpus Annotated with Full Coreference. In *Proceedings of the Eleventh International Conference on Language Resources and Evaluation (LREC 2018)*, Paris, France. European Language Resources Association (ELRA).

Ekaterina Lapshinova-Koltunski, Sharid Loáiciga, Christian Hardmeier, and Pauline Krielke. 2019. Cross-lingual Incongruences in the Annotation of Coreference. In *Proceedings of the Second Workshop on Computational Models of Reference, Anaphora and Coreference*, pages 26–34, Minneapolis, USA. Association for Computational Linguistics.

Sharid Loáiciga, Sara Stymne, Preslav Nakov, Christian Hardmeier, Jörg Tiedemann, Mauro Cettolo, and Yannick Versley. 2017. Findings of the 2017 DiscoMT Shared Task on Cross-lingual Pronoun Prediction. In *Proceedings of the Third Workshop on Discourse in Machine Translation*, pages 1–16.

Christopher D. Manning, Mihai Surdeanu, John Bauer, Jenny Finkel, Steven J. Bethard, and David McClosky. 2014. The Stanford CoreNLP Natural Language Processing Toolkit. In *Association for Computational Linguistics (ACL) System Demonstrations*, pages 55–60.

Eva Martínez, Carles Creus, Cristina España-Bonet, and Lluís Màrquez. 2017. Using Word Embeddings to Enforce Document-Level Lexical Consistency in Machine Translation. *The 20th Annual Conference of the European Association for Machine Translation. The Prague Bulletin of Mathematical Linguistics*, 108:85–96.

Eva Martínez, Cristina España-Bonet, and Lluís Màrquez. 2014. Document-level Machine Translation as a Re-translation Process. *Procesamiento del Lenguaje Natural (SEPLN)*, 53:103–110.

Sameen Maruf and Gholamreza Haffari. 2018. Document Context Neural Machine Translation with Memory Networks. In *Proceedings of the 56th Annual Meeting of the Association for Computational Linguistics (Volume 1: Long Papers)*, pages 1275–1284, Melbourne, Australia. Association for Computational Linguistics.

Lesly Miculicich, Dhananjay Ram, Nikolaos Pappas, and James Henderson. 2018. Document-Level Neural Machine Translation with Hierarchical Attention Networks. In *Proceedings of the 2018 Conference on Empirical Methods in Natural Language Processing*, pages 2947–2954, Brussels, Belgium. Association for Computational Linguistics.

Lesly Miculicich Werlen and Andrei Popescu-Belis. 2017. Using Coreference Links to Improve Spanish-to-English Machine Translation. In *Proceedings of the 2nd Workshop on Coreference Resolution Beyond OntoNotes (CORBON 2017)*, pages 30–40, Valencia, Spain. Association for Computational Linguistics.

Christoph Müller and Michael Strube. 2006. Multi-Level Annotation of Linguistic Data with MMAX2. *English Corpus Linguistics, Vol.3*, pages 197–214.

Michael Novák and Anna Nedoluzhko. 2015. Correspondences between Czech and English Coreferential Expressions. *Discours*, 16.

Michal Novák. 2018. *Coreference from the Cross-lingual Perspective*. Ph.D. thesis, Univerzita Karlova, Matematicko-fyzikální fakulta.

Michal Novák and Zdeněk Žabokrtský. 2014. Cross-lingual Coreference Resolution of Pronouns. In *Proceedings of COLING 2014, the 25th International Conference on Computational Linguistics: Technical Papers*, pages 14–24, Dublin, Ireland.

Kishore Papineni, Salim Roukos, Todd Ward, and Wei-Jing Zhu. 2002. BLEU: a Method for Automatic Evaluation of Machine Translation. In *Proceedings of the Association of Computational Linguistics*, pages 311–318.

Dario Stojanovski and Alexander Fraser. 2018. Coreference and Coherence in Neural Machine Translation: A Study Using Oracle Experiments. In *Proceedings of the Third Conference on Machine Translation: Research Papers*, pages 49–60, Belgium, Brussels. Association for Computational Linguistics.

Dario Stojanovski and Alexander Fraser. 2019. Improving Anaphora Resolution in Neural Machine Translation Using Curriculum Learning. In *Proceedings of the Machine Translation Summit 2019*, Dublin, Ireland.

Elke Teich. 2003. *Cross-Linguistic Variation in System und Text. A Methodology for the Investigation of Translations and Comparable Texts*. Mouton de Gruyter, Berlin.

Jörg Tiedemann and Yves Scherrer. 2017. Neural Machine Translation with Extended Context. In *Proceedings of the Third Workshop on Discourse in Machine Translation*, pages 82–92, Copenhagen, Denmark. Association for Computational Linguistics.

Zhaopeng Tu, Yang Liu, Shuming Shi, and Tong Zhang. 2018. Learning to remember translation history with a continuous cache. *Transactions of the Association for Computational Linguistics*, 6:407–420.

Ferhan Ture, Douglas W. Oard, and Philip Resnik. 2012. Encouraging Consistent Translation Choices. In *Proceedings of the 2012 Conference of the North*

American Chapter of the Association for Computational Linguistics: Human Language Technologies (NAACL HLT), NAACL HLT '12, pages 417–426, Stroudsburg, PA, USA. Association for Computational Linguistics.

Ashish Vaswani, Noam Shazeer, Niki Parmar, Jakob Uszkoreit, Llion Jones, Aidan N Gomez, Łukasz Kaiser, and Illia Polosukhin. 2017. Attention is all you need. In *Advances in Neural Information Processing Systems 30*, pages 5998–6008. Curran Associates, Inc.

Rob Voigt and Dan Jurafsky. 2012. Towards a Literary Machine Translation: The Role of Referential Cohesion. In *Proceedings of the NAACL-HLT 2012 Workshop on Computational Linguistics for Literature*, pages 18–25, Montréal, Canada. Association for Computational Linguistics.

Elena Voita, Pavel Serdyukov, Rico Sennrich, and Ivan Titov. 2018. Context-Aware Neural Machine Translation Learns Anaphora Resolution. In *Proceedings of the 56th Annual Meeting of the Association for Computational Linguistics (Volume 1: Long Papers)*, pages 1264–1274, Melbourne, Australia. Association for Computational Linguistics.

Longyue Wang, Zhaopeng Tu, Andy Way, and Qun Liu. 2017. Exploiting Cross-Sentence Context for Neural Machine Translation. In *Proceedings of the 2017 Conference on Empirical Methods in Natural Language Processing*, pages 2826–2831, Copenhagen, Denmark. Association for Computational Linguistics.

Bonnie Webber, Andrei Popescu-Belis, and Jörg Tiedemann. 2017. *Proceedings of the Third Workshop on Discourse in Machine Translation*. Association for Computational Linguistics, Copenhagen, Denmark.

Tong Xiao, Jingbo Zhu, Shujie Yao, and Hao Zhang. 2011. Document-level Consistency Verification in Machine Translation. In *Proceedings of the Machine Translation Summit XIII*, pages 131–138.

Deyi Xiong, Min Zhang, and Xing Wang. 2015. Topic-based Coherence Modeling for Statistical Machine Translation. *IEEE Transactions on Audio, Speech, and Language Processing*, 23(3):483–493.

Heike Zinsmeister, Stefanie Dipper, and Melanie Seiss. 2012. Abstract pronominal anaphors and label nouns in German and English: selected case studies and quantitative investigations. *Translation: Computation, Corpora, Cognition*, 2(1).

Context-Aware Neural Machine Translation Decoding

Eva Martínez Garcia
TALP Research Center,
Universitat Politècnica de Catalunya
Barcelona
emartinez@cs.upc.edu

Carles Creus
Vicomtech
Donostia
ccreus@vicomtech.org

Cristina España-Bonet
Saarland University
DFKI GmbH
Saarbrücken
cristinae@dfki.de

Abstract

This work presents a decoding architecture that fuses the information from a neural translation model and the context semantics enclosed in a semantic space language model based on word embeddings. The method extends the beam search decoding process and therefore can be applied to any neural machine translation framework. With this, we sidestep two drawbacks of current document-level systems: (*i*) we do not modify the training process so there is no increment in training time, and (*ii*) we do not require document-level annotated data. We analyze the impact of the fusion system approach and its parameters on the final translation quality for English–Spanish. We obtain consistent and statistically significant improvements in terms of BLEU and METEOR and observe how the fused systems are able to handle synonyms to propose more adequate translations as well as help the system to disambiguate among several translation candidates for a word.

1 Introduction

Neural Machine Translation (NMT) systems represent the current state-of-the-art for machine translation technologies and even some evaluations claim that they have reached human performance (Hassan et al., 2018). These systems typically translate documents sentence by sentence, ignoring in the process inter-sentence context and document-level information, and this fact limits the maximum quality that they can achieve. Läubli et al. (2018) show how human translations are preferred over machine translations when they are evaluated at document level, even if the opposite happens at sentence level.

Although there exist several approaches that successfully enhance state-of-the-art neural machine translation systems to take into account document-level information, these systems usually propose modifications to the neural architecture (Wang et al., 2017a; Jean et al., 2017; Voita et al., 2018; Tu et al., 2018; Maruf and Haffari, 2018; Miculicich Werlen et al., 2018; Jean and Cho, 2019) making the training process slower, or require the training data to be annotated with document-level information, such as the document boundaries (Tiedemann and Scherrer, 2017; Junczys-Dowmunt, 2019; Talman et al., 2019; España-Bonet et al., 2019). The main benefit of these approaches is that the neural translation models they obtain are better tuned and able to handle document-level information. However, the training data with the document-level annotations that they require is still scarce, and also, their design increments the training times since the complexity of their neural architectures increase the model parameters to learn.

We propose an alternative to introducing inter-sentence information in an NMT system that follows the encoder–decoder architecture with attention of Bahdanau et al. (2015) without changing the neural translation model architecture. Furthermore, our approach does not need a costly training process with scarce document-level tagged data. Roughly, we modify the beam search algorithm to allow the introduction of a Semantic Space Language Model (SSLM) (Hardmeier et al., 2012) working in shallow fusion (Gülçehre et al., 2017) with a pre-trained NMT model. When evaluated on English–Spanish translations, we observe promising improvements in the automatic evaluation metrics used for the analysis.

The paper is organized as follows. Section 2 revisits the related work. We present the particularities of our approach in Section 3. We describe the experiments and results in Section 4, including an evaluation with oracles to assess the potential impact of our techniques, and conclude in Section 5.

Proceedings of the Fourth Workshop on Discourse in Machine Translation (DiscoMT 2019), pages 13–23
Hong Kong, China, November 3, 2019.

2 Related Work

The interest in making NMT systems able to include wider context information in the translation process has increased in recent years (Jean et al., 2017; Popescu-Belis, 2019), and even in some cases the *necessity* for exploring new approaches of document-level machine translation has been argued (Läubli et al., 2018).

On the one hand, several approaches tried to extend the context beyond the sentence information by modifying the system's input. Tiedemann and Scherrer (2017) concatenate the previous source sentence to the current one, whereas Bawden et al. (2018) also concatenate the previous predicted target sentence.

On the other hand, more sophisticated context-aware approaches propose to modify the NMT architecture. Jean et al. (2017) propose a variation of an attentional recurrent NMT system (Bahdanau et al., 2015) by including an additional encoder and attentional model to encode as context sentence the previous source sentence, showing how NMT systems can also benefit from larger contexts. Wang et al. (2017a) propose a cross-sentence context-aware approach that integrates the historical contextual information within the NMT system. However, these approaches only extend the source context but ignore the target side context. In contrast, Tu et al. (2018) take into account the target side context by using a lightweight cache-like memory network which stores bilingual hidden representations as translation history. More recent approaches implement system extensions that handle both source and target side contexts. Maruf and Haffari (2018) use memory networks to capture global source and target document context. Also, Maruf et al. (2019) present an approach to selectively focus on relevant sentences in the document context and not only consider a few previous sentences as context.

There are other approaches that study the effect of introducing context information within Transformer-based translation systems. Voita et al. (2018) present a variation of the Transformer (Vaswani et al., 2017) that extends the handled context by taking in the input both the current and previous sentences. Miculicich Werlen et al. (2018) extend it by integrating a hierarchical attention model to capture inter-sentence connections, Jean and Cho (2019) by including a context-aware regularization, and Zhang et al. (2018) propose to use a new context encoder to represent document-level context in combination with the original Transformer encoder-decoder architecture.

The importance of document-level translation is also seen in the recent WMT2019[1] news translation shared task, where for the first time a specific track for document-level MT was included. The systems presented at the shared task follow the previously explained strategies: introducing the inter-sentence context information into the NMT system by augmenting the training data including document-level information, i.e., including coreference information (España-Bonet et al., 2019), or just by increasing the training-sequence length in order to capture a larger data context (Popel et al., 2019; Talman et al., 2019; Junczys-Dowmunt, 2019), or introducing variations in the NMT architecture to take into account document-level information (Stahlberg et al., 2019; Talman et al., 2019).

Also related to our work, but far from machine translation, is the work by Wang and Cho (2016). They present an approach to include document-level context into language modeling by implementing fusion approaches that help the LSTM maintain separated the inter- and the intra-sentence context dependencies. Their conclusions show how using a wider context helps neural language models. We borrow the idea of (shallow) fusion and apply it to neural machine translation. In this line, Ji et al. (2015) presented new language models able to capture contextual information within and beyond the sentence level.

3 Context-Aware Decoding

Our document-level extension of the NMT decoding process benefits from the shallow fusion technique. In particular, it exploits the flexibility of being able to combine a general NMT model with a more domain specific Language Model (LM) to guide the NMT system towards a more adequate translation. In our approach, this other model is an SSLM used to introduce inter-sentence context information into the NMT decoding process. In the remaining of this section we briefly describe the SSLM (Section 3.1), the shallow fusion technique (Section 3.2), and finalize detailing our proposed combination (Section 3.3).

[1] `http://www.statmt.org/wmt19/translation-task.html`

3.1 Semantic Space Language Model (SSLM)

A semantic space language model is a probabilistic model able to predict the following word on a sequence taking into account the semantics, and so able to score the semantic relationship among a bunch of words in a sequence. In particular, we follow the SSLM definition presented by Hardmeier et al. (2012), who describe an SSLM based on a word dense vector model built with latent semantic analysis (Foltz et al., 1998; Bellegarda, 2000) and the cosine similarity, which is converted into a probability by a histogram lookup, as proposed by Bellegarda (2000). However, we substitute their LSA model for a word vector model built on the CBOW implementation of the WORD2VEC toolkit (Mikolov et al., 2013).

Intuitively, an SSLM mimics a traditional n-gram language model, but it is computed over semantic information and its expected effect is to promote translation choices that are semantically similar to the target context. To this end, for each candidate word w to append to the target translation, a score is computed based on the cosine similarity between the vector representation of w and the sum of the vector representations of the n target words that precede w in the document translation. In our system, the non-content words and the words unknown to the model are handled specially, both when computing their associated score and when considering them as part of the context of any later word. More precisely, given an already generated word sequence $y_{k-1} = w_1 w_2 \dots w_{k-1}$, the score associated by the SSLM to a translation candidate w_k proposed to extend the translation sequence, denoted $p_{SSLM}(w_k|y_{k-1})$, is:

$$\begin{cases} p_{uni}(w_k) & \text{if } w_k \text{ is a SW} \\ \alpha\, sim(\vec{c}_{y_{k-1}}, \mu(w_k)) & \text{if } w_k \in \text{dom}(\mu) \text{ is not SW} \\ \varepsilon & \text{otherwise} \end{cases}$$

where p_{uni} maps each stop word (SW) to its relative frequency in the training corpus, α is the proportion of content words in the training corpus, $\vec{c}_{y_{k-1}}$ is the vector representing the preceding context of w_k (i.e., the sum of the vector representations of the last n non-stop known words of y_{k-1}), sim of two vectors is their cosine similarity linearly scaled to the range $[0, 1]$, i.e.,

$$sim(\vec{a}, \vec{b}) = \frac{1}{2} \frac{\vec{a} \cdot \vec{b}}{||\vec{a}|| ||\vec{b}||} + \frac{1}{2},$$

the word vector model is represented by μ and maps words to their associated vector representations, with $\text{dom}(\mu)$ being its domain, and ε is a small fixed probability. Note that the lower bound 0 of sim corresponds to the case where the vectors are diametrically opposed (semantically distant) whereas the upper bound 1 to the case where they have the same orientation (semantically close). We use the value $n = 30$ chosen by Hardmeier et al. (2012) to make it possible that the context $\vec{c}_{y_{k-1}}$ used in the computations crosses sentence boundaries. Note that although our system does not need any document-level annotation, it will understand that any set of sentences in its input can be understood as a document. Thus, we need to translate document per document.

3.2 Shallow Fusion

Fusion techniques (Gülçehre et al., 2015, 2017) have shown to be successful in several natural language tasks to merge information from two different neural models. In our context, they are motivated by how Statistical Machine Translation (SMT) systems integrate the information from different feature functions that represent different probabilistic models. There are four main fusion techniques: deep, shallow, cold, and simple fusion. All of them extend the conditional probability learned by one model introducing the information from a second one, where the specific method that is used to combine both models is the main differentiator between the approaches.

Deep, cold, and simple fusion are techniques that need to train the resulting fused network. Deep fusion (Gülçehre et al., 2015, 2017; Stahlberg et al., 2018; Sriram et al., 2018) proposes a method to merge a translation model and a language model by introducing a gating mechanism that learns to balance the weight of the additional language model. Cold fusion (Sriram et al., 2018) goes a step beyond and proposes to implement a deep fusion where the NMT model is trained from scratch including the LM as a fixed part of the network. This allows the NMT to better model the conditioning on the source sequence while the target language modeling is covered by the LM. Simple fusion (Stahlberg et al., 2018) is the latest approach. It arises as an alternative simple method to use monolingual data for NMT training. Roughly, it integrates the shallow fusion technique in training time.

Shallow fusion is a simpler approach that fol-

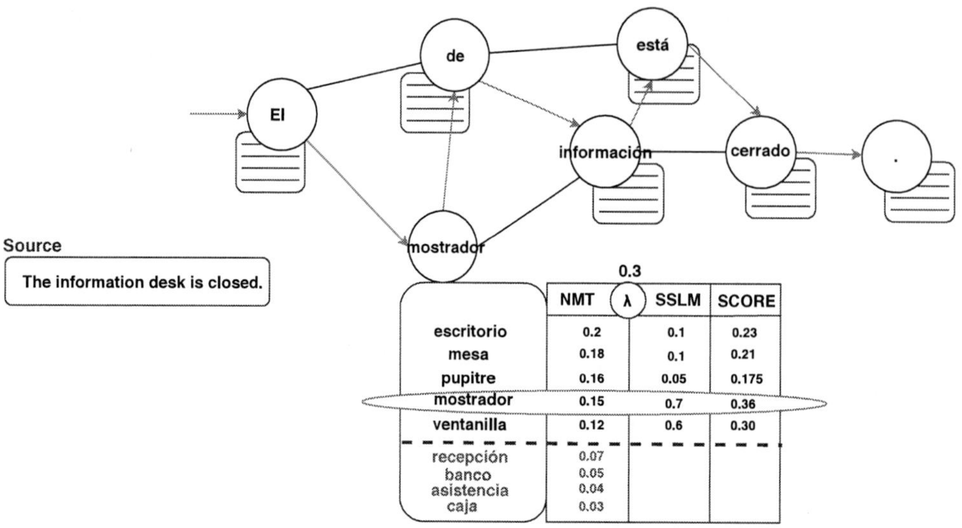

Figure 1: Sketch of the shallow fusion of an SSLM and an NMT inside the beam search algorithm. In this example, the process re-scores the $N = 5$ best candidates from the NMT model using the scores from the SSLM. Directed edges in the graph mark the path found by the beam search that maximizes the translation probability, whereas undirected edges mark possible steps considered by the beam search algorithm.

lows the same idea as deep fusion but, in contrast, proposes the combination of the probabilities from the two models at inference time. To this end, it changes the decoding objective function to integrate an LM prediction. The usual decoding objective function for an MT system with input x can be written as:

$$\hat{y} = \arg\max_{y} \log p(y|x)$$

whereas the shallow fusion variation introduces the LM in a manner inspired by the SMT log-linear model:

$$\hat{y} = \arg\max_{y} \left(\log p(y|x) + \lambda \log p_{LM}(y) \right) \quad (1)$$

where p_{LM} is a language model trained on monolingual target data and λ is its weight. The LM used by Gülçehre et al. (2017) is an LSTM-based RNN language model, but could be any model that generates as output a probability distribution on the discrete space of the target vocabulary shared with the translation model.

An advantage of shallow fusion over the other fusion techniques is that it only needs to adjust the weight λ for the language model by a grid-search on development data, avoiding a long training on large corpora. Furthermore, this technique can be easily applied to any NMT model, either RNN-based or purely attention-based neural models. In the same way as deep fusion, it uses independently pre-trained LM and NMT models. Although this can hinder the system performance, it can also be seen as an advantage due to the flexibility it confers.

3.3 Shallow Fusion between NMT and SSLM

In our model, we substitute the language model probability p_{LM} in the shallow fusion decoding function (Eq. 1) by the SSLM associated probability:

$$\hat{y} = \arg\max_{y} \left(\log p(y|x) + \lambda \log p_{SSLM}(y) \right)$$

Since the computation of p_{SSLM} for each generated word takes into account the preceding context of that word, it is necessary to modify the beam search of the NMT decoder. We implement a cache mechanism to keep track of the context information from the previously generated words, extending beyond sentence boundaries. The cache allows to add together the word embeddings from the previously generated words to obtain $\vec{c}_{y_{k-1}}$.

Additionally, the NMT model requires not only an estimate for a given target word, but a distribution probability over the entire target vocabulary space. Thus, $p_{SSLM}(w_k|y_{k-1})$ must be computed for each word w_k in the target vocabulary. Unfortunately, such an approach would have a high computational cost. Following the ranking/filtering approaches of Jean et al. (2015) and Wang et al. (2017b), we speed up this computation by filtering the words to score by the SSLM. In particular, p_{SSLM} is only computed on the N target words with the highest probabilities from the NMT model, that is, only the N best candidates from the NMT model are considered by the SSLM. Figure 1 depicts how the filtering process works in combination with the shallow fusion of the NMT and the SSLM models during the beam search. Recall that although our system does not need any document-level annotation, it will understand any set of sentences in its input as a document, and thus we translate document per document.

4 Experiments

4.1 Settings

Our baseline NMT model follows the encoder–decoder architecture with attention of Bahdanau et al. (2015) and it is built using the OPENNMT-LUA toolkit (Klein et al., 2017). We use a 4-layered bidirectional RNN encoder and a 4-layered RNN-based decoder with 800-dimensional hidden layers. Word embeddings are set to 500 dimensions for both source and target vocabularies. Stochastic gradient descent is used as optimizer algorithm for training, setting an initial learning rate of 1 and a learning decay of 0.7 after epoch 10 or if there is no loss improvement over the validation set. Training data is distributed on batches of 64 sentences and we use a 0.3 dropout probability between recurrent layers. Finally, a maximum sentence length of 50 tokens is used for both source and target sides and the vocabulary size is 50,000 for both target and source languages. The system is trained on the EUROPARL-V7 parallel corpus, using the NEWSCOMMENTARY2009 corpus as validation set. The system at epoch 20 is to be shallow fused with the SSLM.

We implement the shallow fusion of the SSLM and an NMT as an extension of the attentional encoder–decoder NMT baseline. The Word Vector Models (WVM) used as SSLMs are built using WORD2VEC with the CBOW algorithm (Mikolov et al., 2013), using a context window size of 5 and 600-dimensional vectors. The training data set for this model is the Spanish side of a set of parallel English–Spanish corpora available in OPUS[2] (Tiedemann, 2012, 2009). We select the EUROPARL-V7, UNITED NATIONS, MULTILINGUAL UNITED NATIONS, and SUBTITLES-2012 corpora, which total 759 million words for Spanish. We use NEWSCOMMENTARY2011 as test set. We take advantage of the document annotations from the NEWSCOMMENTARY corpus to translate the test set document by document to avoid addition of random noise.

We evaluate the quality of the outputs with two automatic metrics, BLEU (Papineni et al., 2002) and METEOR (Banerjee and Lavie, 2005).

4.2 Oracle Analysis

We implement three oracles to assess the potential impact of our techniques. The oracles behave as our fused approach, but leverage the reference translation to bias the decoding towards the word choices that are present in the reference. The goal of ORACLE1 and ORACLE2 is to assess the utility of the information enclosed in the WVM used by the SSLM, i.e., to check whether the semantic information of SSLM can help in producing better translations. ORACLE3 mimics our fused decoding approach and its goal is to evaluate the potential gain of using an SSLM in combination with an NMT. In other words, with ORACLE3 we check how much the SSLM can help the NMT disambiguate between its best translation candidates, thus obtaining an upper bound for the improvements that can be achieved by shallow fusing an SSLM and an NMT system.

ORACLE1 proceeds offline as follows: once a sentence has been translated, for each target word t *(i)* it uses the attention information to map that t to its corresponding source word s and, in turn, maps that s to its corresponding target word r found in the reference, and *(ii)* it replaces the target word t by r whenever $t \neq r$ and r is among the M words that are closest to t (w.r.t. cosine similarity) according to our WVM. Note that the use of attention in step *(i)* to map between target and source words is not as straightforward as the alignment information in an SMT system. In particular, we consider that a target word t and a source word s are one-to-one mapped, denoted $t \overset{1}{\leftrightarrow} s$, when the following holds: the attention from t to s is maximal among the attentions from that t to any source word s' and also among the attentions from any

[2] http://opus.lingfil.uu.se/

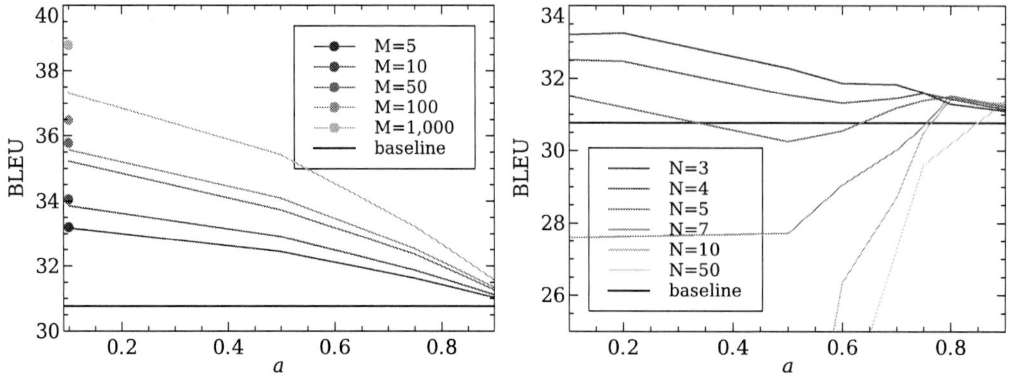

Figure 2: BLEU score of ORACLE1 (left, bullets), ORACLE2 (left, line plots), and ORACLE3 (right, line plots), as a function of the threshold a (ORACLE2 and ORACLE3) and for several values of the parameters M (ORACLE1 and ORACLE2) and N (ORACLE3). For ORACLE1 and ORACLE2, increasing the value of M beyond 1,000 does not affect the obtained scores noticeably.

target word t' to that s, i.e., $t \overset{1}{\leftrightarrow} s$ if and only if $att(t,s) = \max\{att(t',s') : t' = t \vee s' = s\}$, where $att(.,.)$ denotes the attention value between two words. We use an analogous definition for the one-to-one mapping $s \overset{1}{\leftrightarrow} r$ between the source and reference words.[3] Thus, for the target word t in consideration, step (*i*) tries to find the word r of the reference satisfying $t \overset{1}{\leftrightarrow} s \overset{1}{\leftrightarrow} r$, for some source word s. Table 1 and Figure 2 show the results for ORACLE1. We observe that the WVM encodes semantically-valid candidates close together, as there is a noticeable improvement in the BLEU score even when considering just the $M = 5$ closest candidates. Also, the accuracy of the oracle's translations increases with the number M of considered closest words. This is expected since augmenting the number M also increases the coverage of the target vocabulary. In the limit, when M allows to encompass the whole $50K$-word vocabulary, ORACLE1 simply rewrites the translation into the reference as far as the attention information allows, reaching an increase of $+8.02$ in BLEU score.

ORACLE2 works as ORACLE1 but proceeds online with the beam search. That is, when a hypothesis of the beam is to be extended with a new target word t, the oracle (*i*) analyzes the attention information to identify the actual word r used in the reference to translate the source word s that t corresponds to and (*ii*) replaces t with r under the same circumstances as before (i.e., when $t \neq r$ and r appears in the list of M words closest to t according to our WVM). In this occasion, however, the attention information needed in step (*i*) to deduce the one-to-one mappings between the target and source is not fully available, as the target sentence is still being generated. For this reason, we need to add a minimal threshold a for the attention and refine our criterion as $t \overset{1,a}{\longleftrightarrow} s$ if and only if $t \overset{1}{\leftrightarrow} s \wedge att(t,s) \geq a$. Thus, for the target word t in consideration, step (*i*) tries to find the word r of the reference satisfying $t \overset{1,a}{\longleftrightarrow} s \overset{1}{\leftrightarrow} r$, for some source word s. Table 1 and Figure 2 present also the results for ORACLE2. The results are analogous to those of ORACLE1, but with lower scores. This difference of score between both oracles is almost negligible for the smallest values of M and a, but the distance widens as either M or a increases. This shows that our definition of $\overset{1,a}{\longleftrightarrow}$ is a proper approximation to obtain the mappings when not having the full attention information, as the permissive value $a = 0.1$ does not seem to be affected by noisy alignments for low values of M. This is because the oracle only replaces words by other

System	BLEU↑	MTR↑	N	M	a
baseline	30.77	49.86	-	-	-
ORACLE1	38.79	57.85	-	1,000	-
ORACLE2	37.32	54.35	-	1,000	0.1
ORACLE3	33.25	51.74	3	-	0.2

Table 1: BLEU and METEOR (MTR) scores obtained with the oracles defined in Section 4.2.

[3] The mapping from source to reference is done through attention by using the OpenNMT option of passing the target gold standard in the input.

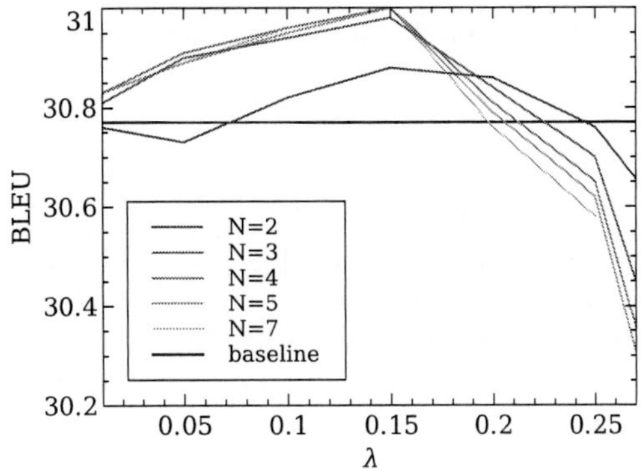

Figure 3: BLEU score of the fused system as a function of the weight λ, for several values of the parameter N.

N	**BLEU↑**	**METEOR↑**	**#unknown**
-	30.77	49.86	5901
2	30.88	50.17	4632
3	† 30.98	50.14	4501
4	† 31.00	50.15	4475
5	† 31.00	50.14	4459
7	† 31.00	50.14	4463
10	† 31.00	50.14	4463

Table 2: BLEU and METEOR scores obtained with the fused systems with $\lambda = 0.15$, together with the amount of unknown words in their output, where the first row corresponds to the baseline. † marks systems that are significantly different to the baseline with a p-value of 0.05, according to bootstrap resampling (Koehn, 2004).

semantically-close words (e.g., by synonyms), and thus, each of the substitutions preserves the meaning of the replaced word even if in some occasions the computed alignment is not adequate. Conversely, by increasing M the oracle handles lists of candidates that are more semantically distant, and thus, in combination with the uncertainty of the alignments, the system introduces more errors.

ORACLE3 proceeds online with the beam search like ORACLE2, just differing on the criterion used to replace the target word t by the corresponding reference word r: the replacement is done when $t \neq r$ and, moreover, r appears among the N best candidates proposed by the NMT model. Note that this oracle does not use in any way the WVM underlying the SSLM: it simply assumes that such model will properly promote the correct word (i.e., the reference word) whenever it is present among the N top candidates of the NMT. Table 1 and Figure 2 present also the results for ORACLE3, which show that there is some margin for improvement for the fused system with respect to the NMT working in isolation. In contrast with ORACLE2, ORACLE3 produces more errors the more candidates that it considers, i.e., the greater the value of N is. Also, considering alignments with lower probabilities only helps when the value of N is small. In particular, considering more candidates by increasing N needs a stronger (i.e., higher) attention threshold a in order to filter out noisy substitutions. Nevertheless, in that more restrictive configuration of a, the results for the various values of N tend to converge.

In summary, ORACLE1 shows that the WVM of the SSLM properly clusters semantically-valid candidates close together, ORACLE2 that incomplete attention information does not hinder the oracle's ability to approximate the alignments, and ORACLE3 that there is a wide enough margin for improvement when fusing the systems.

4.3 System Results and Analysis

Our system has two main hyperparameters: the number N of NMT translation options that are used in the fusion, and the weight of the semantic language model λ. Table 2 and Figure 3 show the results of the automatic evaluation of the different variations of the presented fused system. The figure shows how the maximum quality is achieved around $\lambda = 0.15$, independently of the number N of re-scored candidates. All of our systems are able to improve the baseline for every value of N that we explored, achieving a statistically significant improvement of +0.23 in BLEU score and +0.31 in METEOR. Nevertheless, there is still room for further gains since, as seen in Table 1, ORACLE3 is able to increase +2.48 BLEU and +1.88 METEOR points.

We observe in Table 2 that the scores improve as long as we increase the value of N until it seems to stabilize for $N \geq 4$. Furthermore, comparing the outputs for $\lambda = 0.15$, the translations that the system produces with $N = 4$ only differ in 95 sentences with respect to those for $N = 5$ and in 107 for $N = 7$, while having 1,407 sentences out of 3,003 that differ with respect to the baseline. Also, the translations for $N = 5$ are almost exactly the same as with $N = 7$, differing only in 30 sentences, whereas the translations for $N = 7$ and $N = 10$ coincide. These facts support that the systems with $N \geq 4$ are converging towards an equivalent output. Looking into these differences, we realize that they manage different synonyms that may or not be in the reference. Like translating *"I have to"* as *"Tengo"* or *"Voy a tener"* which can be equivalent depending on the context.

We also observe that with larger values of N, the translations tend to be noisier or less adequate with respect to the source. For instance, *"Offices need a kindergarten nearby, architects have understood."* is translated as:

"las Oficinas necesitan una guardería cercana, los arquitectos han comprendido" (N=4)

"las oficinas de las oficinas de asistencia necesitan una guardería cercana." (N=7)

Notice in the second one the useless repetition of the translation for *"Offices"* and the appearance of the extra concept of assistance (*"asistencia"*) that does not appear in the source sentence. Also, the information regarding the architects is missing in the second translation. Two important error types in NMT systems, word omission and new word creation, are exacerbated with large values for N.

Another example of more accurate translation occurs when translating *"According to Meteo France"*. The best system using $N \geq 5$ translates this as *"Según Francia"* losing the reference to the meteorological company. In contrast, using $N = 4$, the system is able to generate a more accurate translation *"Según Meteo Francia"*. This analysis reflects the noise introduced by increasing the number of re-scored translation candidates by the system. In other words, it is important to have enough candidates to see more adequate translations, but there is a trade-off that the system needs to maintain between the number of new options and the noise introduced by these re-scored options.

Finally, we observe that the increase in the translation quality is also related to the decrease in the number of unknown words generated by the system. Since we use complete tokens without BPE (Sennrich et al., 2016) or SENTENCEPIECE (Kudo and Richardson, 2018) as translation units, several tokens are unknowns to the system. In general, the number of generated unknown words with the shallow fusion approach drops almost a 25% with respect to the unknown words generated by the baseline. For instance, the worst case-scenario sentence *"I'm rather a novice in Prague politics responded Lukas Kaucky."* is translated by the baseline as:

"Más bien soy un $\langle$*unk*$\rangle$ *en la política de Praga,* $\langle$*unk*$\rangle$ *a Lucas* $\langle$*unk*$\rangle$*."*

whereas our fused system is able to produce:

"Más bien soy un ***novato*** *en la política de Praga,* ***respondió*** *a Lucas* $\langle$*unk*$\rangle$*."*

generating good translations for *"novice"* and *"responded"*. These examples illustrate how fusing the SSLM with the NMT model helps the latter to disambiguate between the considered translation candidates for a word.

Finally, we pursue a little manual evaluation with 3 native-Spanish speakers with fluent English. We select a common subset of sentences from the test set translated by the baseline NMT and by the fused system with $N = 4$ and $\lambda = 0.15$. We randomly choose 100 sentences with at least 5 and at most 30 words with different translations. The annotators were asked for each of the 100 selected sentences to rank the output of both systems according to their general translation quality, allowing to rank them as tying. System outputs were presented in random order to avoid system identification. The annotators find 49% of the time that the translation from the fused system is better than the baseline, and they consider the quality of both translations to tie 19% of the time. They agreed 67.33% of the time, reaching a $\kappa = 0.4733$ (Fleiss, 1971) showing a "moderate" inter-annotator agreement (Landis and Koch, 1977). These results support that fused systems are able to improve the translations' quality.

5 Summary and Conclusions

We presented a new approach that extends NMT decoding by introducing information from the preceding context on the target side. It fuses an attentional RNN with an SSLM by modifying the computation of the final score for an element of the target vocabulary inside the beam search algorithm. It is a flexible approach since it is compatible with any NMT architecture, and it allows to combine pre-trained models.

We reach improvements in the BLEU and METEOR scores of up to +0.23 and +0.31 respectively for English-to-Spanish translations. We analyze the impact of the different parameters of the system on these scores, observing that it is important to maintain a trade-off between the number of re-scored candidates, the SSLM weight, and the noise that will be introduced in the final translations. It is remarkable that our systems are able to propose valid translations where the baseline fails to choose one, making the number of unknown words drop while the translation quality increases. Also, a small manual evaluation shows that humans tend to prefer fused system outputs.

As future work, we find interesting to pursue an in-depth manual evaluation to analyze how end users perceive the variations produced by our systems. The next step will be to test this implementation within Transformer-based NMT systems (Vaswani et al., 2017) to analyze how the inter-sentence information can affect the quality of attention-based translation systems and also to use BPEed input to compare the positive effect on unknown words that we observed. These two studies will improve the quality of the systems as a whole (both baseline and fused). In order to better capture the improvements reachable by our oracles, we want to analyse the validity of the cosine similarity as a measure and use other alternatives such as CSLS (cross-domain similarity local scaling) (Lample et al., 2018), or other margin-based scores instead (Artetxe and Schwenk, 2019).

Finally, we are interested in making a thorougher evaluation of the domain adaptation power of this technique by carrying out experiments designed to show how an embedding model trained on several specific domain data can guide a general-oriented NMT system towards more specific and adequate translations.

Acknowledgments

The project on which this paper is based was partially funded by the German Federal Ministry of Education and Research under the funding code 01IW17001 (Deeplee). Responsibility for the content of this publication is with the authors.

References

Mikel Artetxe and Holger Schwenk. 2019. Margin-based parallel corpus mining with multilingual sentence embeddings. In *Proceedings of the 57th Conference of the Association for Computational Linguistics (ACL) – Volume 1*, pages 3197–3203.

Dzmitry Bahdanau, Kyunghyun Cho, and Yoshua Bengio. 2015. Neural machine translation by jointly learning to align and translate. In *Proceedings of the 3rd International Conference on Learning Representations (ICLR)*.

Satanjeev Banerjee and Alon Lavie. 2005. METEOR: An automatic metric for MT evaluation with improved correlation with human judgments. In *Proceedings of the Workshop on Intrinsic and Extrinsic Evaluation Measures for Machine Translation and/or Summarization (IEEvaluation@ACL)*, pages 65–72.

Rachel Bawden, Rico Sennrich, Alexandra Birch, and Barry Haddow. 2018. Evaluating discourse phenomena in neural machine translation. In *Proceedings of the 2018 Conference of the North American Chapter of the Association for Computational Linguistics: Human Language Technologies (NAACL-HLT) – Volume 1*, pages 1304–1313.

Jerome R. Bellegarda. 2000. Exploiting latent semantic information in statistical language modeling. *Proceedings of the IEEE*, 88(8):1279–1296.

Cristina España-Bonet, Dana Ruiter, and Josef van Genabith. 2019. UdS-DFKI participation at WMT 2019: Low-resource (en–gu) and coreference-aware (en–de) systems. In *Proceedings of the Fourth Conference on Machine Translation (WMT) – Volume 2: Shared Task Papers*, pages 382–389.

Joseph L. Fleiss. 1971. Measuring nominal scale agreement among many raters. *Psychological Bulletin*, 76(5):378–382.

Peter W. Foltz, Walter Kintsch, and Thomas K. Landauer. 1998. The measurement of textual coherence with latent semantic analysis. *Discourse Processes*, 25(2–3):285–307.

Çağlar Gülçehre, Orhan Firat, Kelvin Xu, Kyunghyun Cho, Loïc Barrault, Huei-Chi Lin, Fethi Bougares, Holger Schwenk, and Yoshua Bengio. 2015. On using monolingual corpora in neural machine translation. *CoRR*, abs/1503.03535.

Çağlar Gülçehre, Orhan Firat, Kelvin Xu, Kyunghyun Cho, and Yoshua Bengio. 2017. On integrating a language model into neural machine translation. *Computer Speech & Language*, 45:137–148.

Christian Hardmeier, Joakim Nivre, and Jörg Tiedemann. 2012. Document-wide decoding for phrase-based statistical machine translation. In *Proceedings of the 2012 Joint Conference on Empirical Methods in Natural Language Processing and Computational Natural Language Learning (EMNLP-CoNLL)*, pages 1179–1190.

Hany Hassan, Anthony Aue, Chang Chen, Vishal Chowdhary, Jonathan Clark, Christian Federmann, Xuedong Huang, Marcin Junczys-Dowmunt, William Lewis, Mu Li, Shujie Liu, Tie-Yan Liu, Renqian Luo, Arul Menezes, Tao Qin, Frank Seide, Xu Tan, Fei Tian, Lijun Wu, Shuangzhi Wu, Yingce Xia, Dongdong Zhang, Zhirui Zhang, and Ming Zhou. 2018. Achieving human parity on automatic Chinese to English news translation. *CoRR*, abs/1803.05567.

Sébastien Jean and Kyunghyun Cho. 2019. Context-aware learning for neural machine translation. *CoRR*, abs/1903.04715.

Sébastien Jean, Orhan Firat, Kyunghyun Cho, Roland Memisevic, and Yoshua Bengio. 2015. Montreal neural machine translation systems for WMT'15. In *Proceedings of the Tenth Workshop on Statistical Machine Translation (WMT)*, pages 134–140.

Sébastien Jean, Stanislas Lauly, Orhan Firat, and Kyunghyun Cho. 2017. Does neural machine translation benefit from larger context? *CoRR*, abs/1704.05135.

Yangfeng Ji, Trevor Cohn, Lingpeng Kong, Chris Dyer, and Jacob Eisenstein. 2015. Document context language models. *CoRR*, abs/1511.03962.

Marcin Junczys-Dowmunt. 2019. Microsoft translator at WMT 2019: Towards large-scale document-level neural machine translation. In *Proceedings of the Fourth Conference on Machine Translation (WMT) – Volume 2: Shared Task Papers*, pages 424–432.

Guillaume Klein, Yoon Kim, Yuntian Deng, Jean Senellart, and Alexander M. Rush. 2017. OpenNMT: Open-source toolkit for neural machine translation. In *Proceedings of the 55th Annual Meeting of the Association for Computational Linguistics: System Demonstrations (ACL)*, pages 67–72.

Philipp Koehn. 2004. Statistical significance tests for machine translation evaluation. In *Proceedings of the Conference on Empirical Methods in Natural Language Processing (EMNLP)*, pages 388–395.

Taku Kudo and John Richardson. 2018. SentencePiece: A simple and language independent subword tokenizer and detokenizer for neural text processing. In *Proceedings of the 2018 Conference on Empirical Methods in Natural Language Processing (EMNLP)*, pages 66–71.

Guillaume Lample, Alexis Conneau, Marc'Aurelio Ranzato, Ludovic Denoyer, and Hervé Jégou. 2018. Word translation without parallel data. In *Proceedings of the 6th International Conference on Learning Representations (ICLR)*.

John Richard Landis and Gary Grove Koch. 1977. The measurement of observer agreement for categorical data. *Biometrics*, 33(1):159–174.

Samuel Läubli, Rico Sennrich, and Martin Volk. 2018. Has machine translation achieved human parity? A case for document-level evaluation. In *Proceedings of the 2018 Conference on Empirical Methods in Natural Language Processing (EMNLP)*, pages 4791–4796.

Sameen Maruf and Gholamreza Haffari. 2018. Document context neural machine translation with memory networks. In *Proceedings of the 56th Annual Meeting of the Association for Computational Linguistics (ACL) – Volume 1*, pages 1275–1284.

Sameen Maruf, André F. T. Martins, and Gholamreza Haffari. 2019. Selective attention for context-aware neural machine translation. *CoRR*, abs/1903.08788.

Lesly Miculicich Werlen, Dhananjay Ram, Nikolaos Pappas, and James Henderson. 2018. Document-level neural machine translation with hierarchical attention networks. In *Proceedings of the 2018 Conference on Empirical Methods in Natural Language Processing (EMNLP)*, pages 2947–2954.

Tomas Mikolov, Kai Chen, Gregory S. Corrado, and Jeffrey Dean. 2013. Efficient estimation of word representations in vector space. *CoRR*, abs/1301.3781.

Kishore Papineni, Salim Roukos, Todd Ward, and Wei-Jing Zhu. 2002. BLEU: a method for automatic evaluation of machine translation. In *Proceedings of the 40th Annual Meeting on Association for Computational Linguistics (ACL)*, pages 311–318.

Martin Popel, Dominik Macháček, Michal Auersperger, Ondřej Bojar, and Pavel Pecina. 2019. English-Czech systems in WMT19: Document-level transformer. In *Proceedings of the Fourth Conference on Machine Translation (WMT) – Volume 2: Shared Task Papers*, pages 541–547.

Andrei Popescu-Belis. 2019. Context in neural machine translation: A review of models and evaluations. *CoRR*, abs/1901.09115.

Rico Sennrich, Barry Haddow, and Alexandra Birch. 2016. Neural machine translation of rare words with subword units. In *Proceedings of the 54th Annual Meeting of the Association for Computational Linguistics (ACL) – Volume 1*, pages 1715–1725.

Anuroop Sriram, Heewoo Jun, Sanjeev Satheesh, and Adam Coates. 2018. Cold fusion: Training Seq2Seq models together with language models. In *Proceedings of the 19th Annual Conference of the International Speech Communication Association (Interspeech)*, pages 387–391.

Felix Stahlberg, James Cross, and Veselin Stoyanov. 2018. Simple fusion: Return of the language model. In *Proceedings of the Third Conference on Machine Translation: Research Papers (WMT)*, pages 204–211.

Felix Stahlberg, Danielle Saunders, Adrià de Gispert, and Bill Byrne. 2019. CUED@WMT19:EWC&LMs. In *Proceedings of the Fourth Conference on Machine Translation (WMT) – Volume 2: Shared Task Papers*, pages 563–572.

Aarne Talman, Umut Sulubacak, Raúl Vázquez, Yves Scherrer, Sami Virpioja, Alessandro Raganato, Arvi Hurskainen, and Jörg Tiedemann. 2019. The University of Helsinki submissions to the WMT19 news translation task. In *Proceedings of the Fourth Conference on Machine Translation (WMT) – Volume 2: Shared Task Papers*, pages 611–622.

Jörg Tiedemann. 2009. News from OPUS – A collection of multilingual parallel corpora with tools and interfaces. *Recent Advances in Natural Language Processing (RANLP)*, 5:237–248.

Jörg Tiedemann. 2012. Parallel data, tools and interfaces in OPUS. In *Proceedings of the 8th International Conference on Language Resources and Evaluation (LREC)*, pages 2214–2218.

Jörg Tiedemann and Yves Scherrer. 2017. Neural machine translation with extended context. In *Proceedings of the Third Workshop on Discourse in Machine Translation (DiscoMT@EMNLP)*, pages 82–92.

Zhaopeng Tu, Yang Liu, Shuming Shi, and Tong Zhang. 2018. Learning to remember translation history with a continuous cache. *Transactions of the Association for Computational Linguistics (TACL)*, 6:407–420.

Ashish Vaswani, Noam Shazeer, Niki Parmar, Jakob Uszkoreit, Llion Jones, Aidan N. Gomez, Łukasz Kaiser, and Illia Polosukhin. 2017. Attention is all you need. In *Proceedings of the 31st Annual Conference on Neural Information Processing Systems (NIPS)*, pages 6000–6010.

Elena Voita, Pavel Serdyukov, Rico Sennrich, and Ivan Titov. 2018. Context-aware neural machine translation learns anaphora resolution. In *Proceedings of the 56th Annual Meeting of the Association for Computational Linguistics (ACL) – Volume 1*, pages 1264–1274.

Longyue Wang, Zhaopeng Tu, Andy Way, and Qun Liu. 2017a. Exploiting cross-sentence context for neural machine translation. In *Proceedings of the 2017 Conference on Empirical Methods in Natural Language Processing (EMNLP)*, pages 2826–2831.

Tian Wang and Kyunghyun Cho. 2016. Larger-context language modelling with recurrent neural network. In *Proceedings of the 54th Annual Meeting of the Association for Computational Linguistics (ACL) – Volume 1*, pages 1319–1329.

Yuguang Wang, Shanbo Cheng, Liyang Jiang, Jiajun Yang, Wei Chen, Muze Li, Lin Shi, Yanfeng Wang, and Hongtao Yang. 2017b. Sogou neural machine translation systems for WMT17. In *Proceedings of the Second Conference on Machine Translation (WMT)*, pages 410–415.

Jiacheng Zhang, Huanbo Luan, Maosong Sun, Feifei Zhai, Jingfang Xu, Min Zhang, and Yang Liu. 2018. Improving the Transformer translation model with document-level context. *CoRR*, abs/1810.03581.

When and Why is Document-level Context Useful in Neural Machine Translation?

Yunsu Kim Duc Thanh Tran Hermann Ney
Human Language Technology and Pattern Recognition Group
RWTH Aachen University, Aachen, Germany
{surname}@cs.rwth-aachen.de

Abstract

Document-level context has received lots of attention for compensating neural machine translation (NMT) of isolated sentences. However, recent advances in document-level NMT focus on sophisticated integration of the context, explaining its improvement with only a few selected examples or targeted test sets. We extensively quantify the causes of improvements by a document-level model in general test sets, clarifying the limit of the usefulness of document-level context in NMT. We show that most of the improvements are not interpretable as utilizing the context. We also show that a minimal encoding is sufficient for the context modeling and very long context is not helpful for NMT.

1 Introduction

Neural machine translation (NMT) (Bahdanau et al., 2015; Vaswani et al., 2017) has been originally developed to work sentence by sentence. Recently, it has been claimed that sentence-level NMT generates document-level errors, e.g. wrong coreference of pronouns/articles or inconsistent translations throughout a document (Guillou et al., 2018; Läubli et al., 2018).

A lot of research addresses these problems by feeding surrounding context sentences as additional inputs to an NMT model. Modeling of the context is usually done with fully-fledged NMT encoders with extensions to consider complex relations between sentences (Bawden et al., 2018; Voita et al., 2018; Zhang et al., 2018; Miculicich et al., 2018; Maruf et al., 2019). Despite the high overhead in modeling, translation metric scores (e.g. BLEU) are often only marginally improved, leaving the evaluation to artificial tests targeted for pronoun resolution (Jean et al., 2017; Tiedemann and Scherrer, 2017; Bawden et al., 2018; Voita et al., 2018, 2019). Even if the metric score gets significantly better, the improvement is limited to specific datasets or explained with only a few examples (Tu et al., 2018; Maruf and Haffari, 2018; Kuang and Xiong, 2018; Cao and Xiong, 2018; Zhang et al., 2018; Maruf et al., 2019).

This paper systematically investigates when and why document-level context improves NMT, asking the following research questions:

- In general, how often is the context utilized in an interpretable way, e.g. coreference?
- Is there any other (non-linguistic) cause of improvements by document-level models?
- Which part of a context sentence is actually meaningful for the improvement?
- Is a long-range context, e.g. in ten consecutive sentences, still useful?
- How much modeling power is necessary for the improvements?

To answer these questions, we conduct an extensive qualitative analysis on non-targeted test sets. According to the analysis, we use only the important parts of the surrounding sentences to facilitate the integration of long-range contexts. We also compare different architectures for the context modeling and check sufficient model complexity for a significant improvement.

Our results show that the improvement in BLEU is mostly from a non-linguistic factor: regularization by reserving parameters for context inputs. We also verify that very long context is indeed not helpful for NMT, and a full encoder stack is not necessary for the improved performance.

2 Document-level NMT

In this section, we review the existing document-level approaches for NMT and describe our strategies to filter out uninteresting words in the context

Proceedings of the Fourth Workshop on Discourse in Machine Translation (DiscoMT 2019), pages 24–34
Hong Kong, China, November 3, 2019.

input. We illustrate with an example of including one previous source sentence as the document-level context, which can be easily generalized also to other context inputs such as target hypotheses (Agrawal et al., 2018; Bawden et al., 2018; Voita et al., 2019) or decoder states (Tu et al., 2018; Maruf and Haffari, 2018; Miculicich et al., 2018).

For the notations, we denote a source sentence by **f** and its encoded representations by H. A subscript distinguishes the previous (pre) and current (cur) sentences. e_i indicates a target token to be predicted at position i, and e_1^{i-1} are already predicted tokens in previous positions. Z denotes encoded representations of a partial target sequence.

2.1 Single-Encoder Approach

The simplest method to include context in NMT is to just modify the input, i.e. concatenate surrounding sentences to the current one and put the extended sentence in a normal sentence-to-sentence model (Tiedemann and Scherrer, 2017; Agrawal et al., 2018). A special token is inserted between context and current sentences to mark sentence boundaries (e.g. _BREAK_).

Figure 1 depicts this approach. Here, a single encoder processes the context and current sentences together as one long input. This requires no change in the model architecture but worsens a fundamental problem of NMT: translating long inputs (Koehn and Knowles, 2017). Apart from the data scarcity of a higher-dimensional input space, it is difficult to optimize the attention component to the long spans (Sukhbaatar et al., 2019).

2.2 Multi-Encoder Approach

Alternatively, multi-encoder approaches encode each additional sentence separately. The model learns representations solely of the context sentences which are then integrated into the baseline model architecture. This tackles the integration of additional sentences on the architecture level, in contrast to the single-encoder approach. In the following, we describe two methods of integrating the encoded context sentences. The descriptions below do not depend on specific types of context encoding; one can use recurrent or self-attentive encoders with a variable number of layers, or just word embeddings without any hidden layers on top of them (Section 3.1).

2.2.1 Integration Outside the Decoder

The first method combines encoder representation of all input sentences before being fed to the decoder (Maruf and Haffari, 2018; Voita et al., 2018; Miculicich et al., 2018; Zhang et al., 2018; Maruf et al., 2019). It attends from the representations of the current sentence (H_{cur}) to those of the previous sentence (H_{pre}), yielding $\bar{H}$. Afterwards, a linear interpolation with gating is applied:

$$g\bar{H} + (1-g)H_{\text{cur}} \quad (1)$$

where $g = \sigma\left(W_g\left[\bar{H}; H_{\text{cur}}\right] + b_g\right)$ is gating activation and W_g, b_g are learnable parameters. This type of integration is depicted in Figure 2. By using such a gating mechanism, the model is capable of learning how much additional context information shall be included.

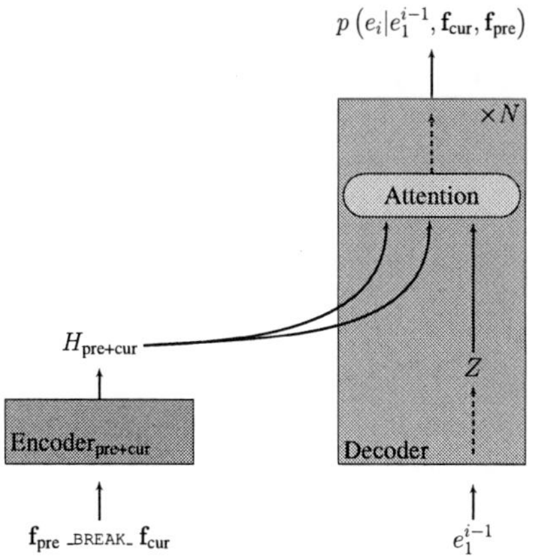

Figure 1: Single-encoder approach.

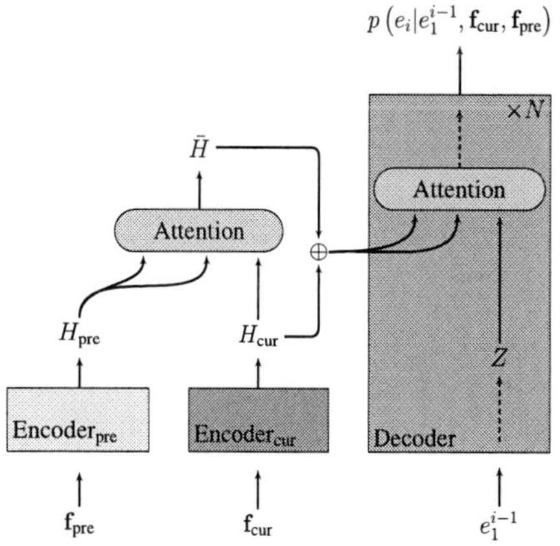

Figure 2: Multi-encoder approach integrating context outside the decoder.

2.2.2 Integration Inside the Decoder

Another method integrates the context inside the decoder; the partial target history e_1^{i-1} is available during the integration. Here, using the (encoded) target history as a query, the decoder attends directly to the context representations. It also has the original attention to the current sentence. Depending on the order of these two attention components, this type of integration has two variants.

Sequential Attentions The first variant is stacking the two attention components, with the output of one component being the query of another (Tu et al., 2018; Zhang et al., 2018).

Figure 3 shows the case when the current sentence is attended by the decoder first, which is then used to attend to the context sentence. This refines the regular attention to the current source sentence with additional context information. The order of the attention components may be switched. To block signals of potentially unimportant context information, a gating mechanism can be employed between the regular and context attention outputs like Section 2.2.1.

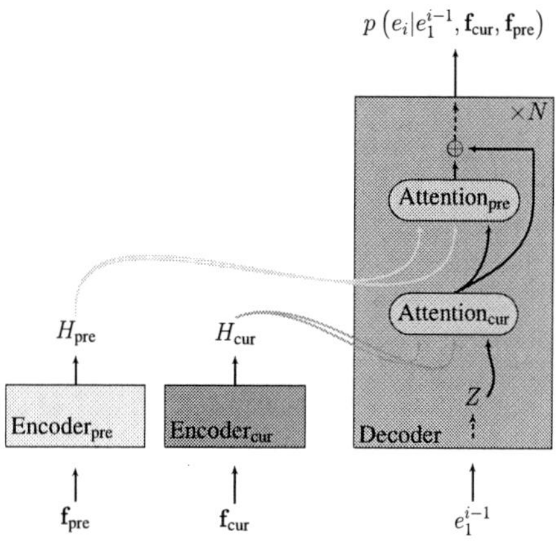

Figure 3: Multi-encoder approach integrating context inside the decoder with sequential attentions.

Parallel Attentions Figure 4 shows the case when performing the two attention operations in parallel and combining them with a gating afterwards (Jean et al., 2017; Cao and Xiong, 2018; Kuang and Xiong, 2018; Bawden et al., 2018; Stojanovski and Fraser, 2018). This method relates document-level context to the target history independently of the current source sentence, and lets the decoding computation faster.

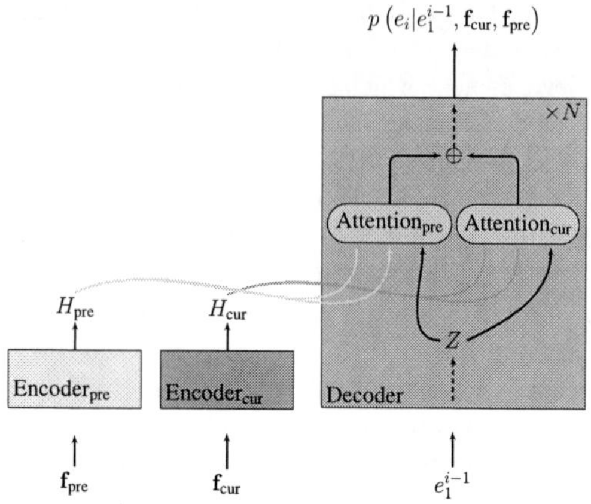

Figure 4: Multi-encoder approach integrating context inside the decoder with parallel attentions.

For each category above, we have described a common architecture shared by previous works in that category. There are slight variations but they do not diverge much from our descriptions.

2.3 Filtering of Words in the Context

Document-level NMT inherently has heavy computations due to longer inputs and additional processing of context. However, intuitively, not all of the words in the context are actually useful in translating the current sentence. For instance, in most literature, the improvements from using document-level context are explained with coreference, which can be resolved with just nouns, articles, and the conjugated words affected by them.

Under the assumption that we do not need the whole context sentence in document-level NMT, we suggest to retain only the context words that are likely to be useful. This makes the training easier with a smaller input space and less memory requirement. Concretely, we filter out words in the context sentences according to pre-defined word lists or predicted linguistic tags:

- Remove stopwords using a pre-defined list[1]
- Remove $n \in \mathbb{N}$ most frequent words
- Retain only named entities
- Retain only the words with specific parts-of-speech (POS) tags

The first method has the same motivation as Kuang et al. (2018) to ignore function words. The second method aims to keep infrequent words that

[1]https://github.com/explosion/spaCy

Original source	in recent years, I correctly foresaw that, in the absence of stronger fiscal stimulus (which was not forthcoming in either Europe or the United States), recovery from the Great Recession of 2008 would be slow.
Remove stopwords	recent years, I correctly foresaw absence stronger fiscal stimulus (forthcoming Europe United States), recovery Great Recession 2008 slow.
Remove most frequent words	recent correctly foresaw absence stronger fiscal stimulus forthcoming either States recovery Great Recession 2008 slow
Retain named entities	recent years Europe the United States the Great Recession 2008
Retain specific POS	years I foresaw the absence stimulus was forthcoming either Europe or the United States recovery the Great Recession 2008 would be

Table 1: Examples for filtering of words in the context (News Commentary v14 English→German).

are domain-specific or containing gender information. We empirically found that $n = 150$ works reasonably well. For the last two methods, we use the FLAIR[2] (Akbik et al., 2018) toolkit. We exclude the tags that are irrelevant to syntax/semantics of the current sentence. The detailed lists of retained tags can be found in the appendix.

The filtering is performed on word level in the preprocessing. When a sentence is completely pruned, we use a special token to denote an empty sentence (e.g. _EMPTY_). Table 1 gives examples of the filtering. We can observe that the original sentence is shortened greatly by removing redundant tokens, but the topic information and the important subjects still remain.

3 Experiments

We evaluate the document-level approaches in IWSLT 2017 English→Italian[3] and WMT 2018 English→German[4] translation tasks. We used TED talk or News Commentary v14 dataset as the training data respectively, preprocessed with the-Moses tokenizer[5] and byte pair encoding (Sennrich et al., 2016) trained with 32k merge operations jointly for source and target languages. In all our experiments, one previous source sentence was given as the document-level context. A special token was inserted at each document boundary, which was also fed as context input when translating sentences around the boundaries. Detailed corpus statistics are given in Table 2.

All experiments were carried out with SOCKEYE (Hieber et al., 2018). We used Adam optimizer (Kingma and Ba, 2015) with the default parameters. The learning rate was reduced by 30% when the perplexity on a validation set was not improving for four checkpoints. When it did not improve for ten checkpoints, we stopped the training. Batch size was 3k tokens, where the bucketing was done for a tuple of current/context sentence lengths. All other settings follow a 6-layer base Transformer model (Vaswani et al., 2017).

In all our experiments, a sentence-level model was pre-trained and used to initialize document-level models, which was crucial for the performance. We also shared the source word embeddings over the original and context encoders.

	en-it	en-de
Running Words	4.3M	8.1M
Sentences	227k	329k
Documents	2,045	8,891
Document Length (avg. #sent)	111	37

Table 2: Training data statistics.

3.1 Model Comparison

Model Architecture Firstly, we compare the performance of existing single-encoder and multi-encoder approaches (Table 3). For each category of document-level methods (Section 2), we test one representative architecture (Figures 2, 3, 4) which encompasses all existing work in that category except slight variations. The tested methods are equal or closest to:

- Single-Encoder: Agrawal et al. (2018)

[2]https://github.com/zalandoresearch/flair
[3]https://sites.google.com/site/iwsltevaluation2017
[4]https://www.statmt.org/wmt18/translation-task.html
[5]http://www.statmt.org/moses

Approach	Context Encoder Architecture	Context Encoder #layers	en-it BLEU [%]	en-it TER [%]	en-de BLEU [%]	en-de TER [%]
Baseline	·	·	31.4	56.1	28.9	61.8
Single-Encoder	Transformer	6	31.5	57.2	28.9	61.4
Multi-Encoder (Out.)	Transformer	6	31.3	56.1	29.1	61.4
Multi-Encoder (Seq.)	Transformer	6	32.6	55.2	29.9	60.7
Multi-Encoder (Para.)	Transformer	6	**32.7**	**54.7**	30.1	60.3
		2	32.6	55.2	30.2	60.5
		1	32.2	55.8	30.0	60.4
	Word Embedding	·	32.5	54.8	**30.3**	**59.9**

Table 3: Comparison of document-level model architectures and complexity.

- Integration outside the decoder: Voita et al. (2018) without sharing the encoder hidden layers over current/context sentences
- Integration inside the decoder
  - Sequential attention: Decoder integration of Zhang et al. (2018) with the order of attentions (current/context) switched
  - Parallel attention: Gating version of Bawden et al. (2018)

The training of the single-encoder method was quite unstable. It took about twice as long as other document-level models, yet yielding no improvements, which is consistent with Kuang and Xiong (2018). Longer inputs make the encoder-decoder attention widely scattered and harder to optimize. We might need larger training data, massive pre-training, and much larger batches to train the single-encoder approach effectively (Junczys-Dowmunt, 2019); however, these conditions are often not realistic.

For the multi-encoder models, if the context is integrated outside the decoder ("Out."), it barely improves upon the baseline. By letting the decoder directly access context sentences with a separate attention component, they all outperform the single-encoder method, improving the sentence-level baseline up to +1.4% BLEU and -1.9% TER. Particularly, when attending to current and context sentences in parallel ("Para."), it provides more flexible and selective information flow from multiple source sentences to the decoder, thus producing better results than the sequential attentions ("Seq.").

Model Complexity In the linguistic sense, surrounding sentences are useful in translating the current sentence mostly by providing case distinctions of nouns or topic information (Section 4). The sequential relation of tokens in the surrounding sentences is important for neither of them. Therefore we investigate how many levels of sequential encoding is actually needed for the improvement by the context. From a 6-layer Transformer encoder, we gradually reduce the model complexity of the context encoder: 2-layer, 1-layer, and only using word embeddings without any sequential encoding. We remove positional encoding (Vaswani et al., 2017) when we encode only with word embeddings.

The results are shown in the lower part of Table 3. Context encoding without any sequential modeling (the last row) shows indeed comparable performance to using a full 6-layer encoder. This simplified encoding eases the memory-intensive document-level training by having 22% fewer model parameters, which allows us to adopt a larger batch size without accumulating gradients. For the remainder of this paper, we stick to using the multi-encoder approach with parallel attention components in the decoder and restricting the context encoding to only word embeddings.

3.2 Filtering Words in the Context

To make the context modeling even lighter, we analyze the effectiveness of the filtered context (Section 2.3) in Table 4. All filtering methods shrink the context input drastically without a significant loss of performance. Each method has its own motivation to retain only useful tokens in the

Context sentence	en-it BLEU [%]	en-it TER [%]	en-de BLEU [%]	en-de TER [%]	#tokens
None	31.4	56.1	28.9	61.8	-
Full sentence	32.5	54.8	30.3	59.9	100%
Remove stopwords	32.2	55.2	30.3	59.9	63%
Remove most frequent words	32.1	55.6	30.2	60.2	51%
Retain only named entities	32.3	55.4	30.3	60.3	**13%**
Retain specific POS	**32.5**	**55.2**	**30.4**	**60.0**	59%

Table 4: Comparison of context word filtering methods.

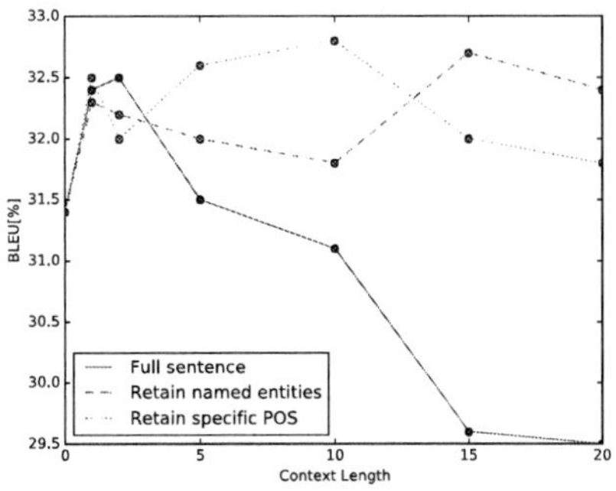

(a) IWSLT **en-it**

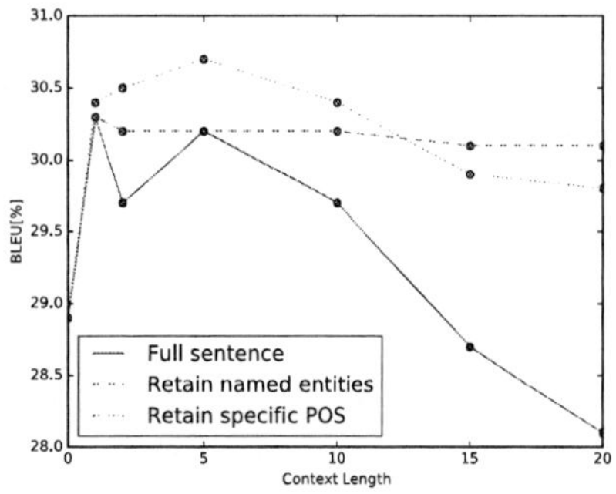

(b) WMT **en-de**

Figure 5: Translation performance as a function of document-level context length (in the number of sentences).

context; the results show that they are all reasonable in practice. In particular, using only named entities as context input, we achieve the same level of improvement with only 13% of tokens in the full context sentences. By filtering words in the context sentences, we can use more examples in each batch for a robust training.

3.3 Context Length

Filtered context inputs (Section 3.2) with a minimal encoding (Section 3.1) make it also feasible to include much longer context without much difficulty. Most of previous works on document-level NMT have not examined context inputs longer than three sentences.

Figure 5 shows the translation performance with an increasing number of context sentences. If we concatenate full context sentences (plain curves), the performance deteriorates severely. We found that it is hard to fit such long sequences in memory as the training becomes very erratic.

The training is much more stable with filtered context; the dashed/dotted curves do not drop significantly even when using 20 context sentences. In the English→Italian task, the performance slightly improves up to 15 context sentences. In the English→German task, there is no improvement by extending the context length over 5 sentences. This discrepancy can be explained with document lengths in each dataset (Table 2). The TED talk corpus for English→Italian has much longer documents, thus it is probable to benefit from larger context windows. However, in general we observe only marginal improvements by enlarging the context length to more than one sentence, as seen also in Bawden et al. (2018), Miculicich et al. (2018), or Zhang et al. (2018).

4 Analysis

Simplifying the context encoder (Section 3.1) and filtering the context input (Section 3.2) are both inspired by the intuition that only a small part of the context is useful for NMT. In order to verify this intuition rigorously, we conduct an extensive analysis on how document-level context helps the translation process, manually checking every output of sentence-level/document-level NMT models; automatic metrics are inherently not suitable for distinguishing document-level behavior. Our analysis is not constrained to certain discourse phenomena which are favored in evaluating document-level models. We quantify various causes of the improvements 1) regardless of its linguistic interpretability and 2) in a realistic scenario where not all the test examples require document-level context. Here are the steps we take:

1. Translate a test set with a sentence-level baseline and a document-level model.
2. Compute per-sentence TER scores of outputs from both models.
3. Select those cases where the document-level model improves the per-sentence TER over the sentence-level baseline.
4. Examine each case of 3 by looking at:
   - Source, context, and translation outputs
   - Attention distribution over the context tokens for each target token: averaged over all decoder layers/heads
   - Gating activation (Equation 1)
5. Classify each case into "coreference", "topic-aware lexical choice", or "not interpretable".

Statistics of each category on the test sets are reported in Table 5. The manual inspection of translation outputs is done by a native-level speaker of Italian or German, respectively.

Only a couple of cases belong to coreference, which is ironically the most advocated improvement in the literature on document-level NMT. One of them is shown in Table 6a. In the document-level NMT, the English word "said" is translated to a correct conjugation of "sagen" (= say) for the third person noun "der Präsident" (= the President). This can be explained by the high attention energy on "Trump" (Figure 7a) in the context sentence.

Another interpretable cause is topic-aware lexical choice (Table 6b). The document-level model actively attends to "seized" and "cocaine" in the context sentence (Figure 7b), and does not miss the source word "raids" in the translation ("Razzien"). When it corrects the translation of polysemous words, it is related to word sense disambiguation (Gonzales et al., 2017; Marvin and Koehn, 2018; Pu et al., 2018). This category includes also a coherence of text style in the translation outputs, depending on the context topic.

	#cases	
Category	**en-it**	**en-de**
Coreference	21	2
Topic-aware lexical choice	66	33
Not interpretable	292	1,211
Total TER improved	379	1,246
Total	1,147	2,998

Table 5: Causes of improvements by document-level context.

We found that only 7.5% of the TER-improved cases can be interpreted as utilizing document-level context. The other cases are mostly general improvements in adequacy or fluency which are not related to the given context. Table 6c shows such an example. It improves the translation by a long-range reordering and rephrasing some nouns, whose clues do not exist in the previous source sentence. Its attention distribution over the context words is totally random and blurry (Figure 7c).

A possible reason for the non-interpretable improvements is regularization of the model, since the training data of our experiments are relatively small. Figure 6 shows that, for most of the improved cases, the model has non-negligible gating activation towards document-level context, even if the output seems not to benefit from the context. It means that, when combining the encoded representations of context/current sentences, the model can reserve some of its capacity to the information from context inputs. This might effectively mitigate overfitting to the given training data.

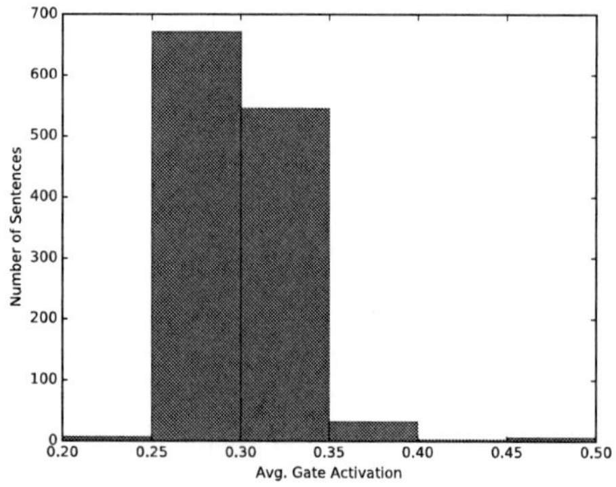

Figure 6: Gating activation for all TER-improved cases of the English→German task, averaged over all layers and target positions.

Previous src	inside the White House, Trump addressed Sikorsky representatives, joking with the media about his own fleet of company products.
Current src	"I know Sikorsky very well," the President said, "I have three of them."
Reference	„ich kenne Sikorsky sehr gut", sagte der Präsident, „ich habe drei davon."
Sent-level hyp	„ich kenne Sikorsky sehr gut", **so** der Präsident, „habe drei davon."
Doc-level hyp	„ich kenne Sikorsky sehr gut," **sagte** der Präsident, „ich habe drei davon".

(a) Coreference

Previous src	in addition, officials seized large quantities of marijuana and cocaine, firearms and several hundred thousand euros.
Current src	at simultaneous raids in Italy, two people were detained.
Reference	bei zeitgleichen Razzien in Italien wurden zwei Personen festgenommen.
Sent-level hyp	gleichzeitig wurden in Italien zwei Personen verhaftet.
Doc-level hyp	bei gleichzeitigen **Razzien** in Italien wurden zwei Menschen inhaftiert.

(b) Topic-aware lexical choice

Previous src	other cities poach good officials and staff members and offer attractive conditions.
Current src	the talk is of a downright "contest between public employers".
Reference	die Rede ist von einem regelrechten „Wettbewerb der öffentlichen Arbeitgeber".
Sent-level hyp	das Gerede ber einen „Wettkampf zwischen öffentlichen Arbeitgebern" ist von einem Gerechtigkeitstreit.
Doc-level hyp	die Rede ist von einem herben „Wettbewerb zwischen öffentlichen Arbeitgebern".

(c) Not interpretable

Table 6: Example translation outputs for each analysis category (WMT English→German newstest2018).

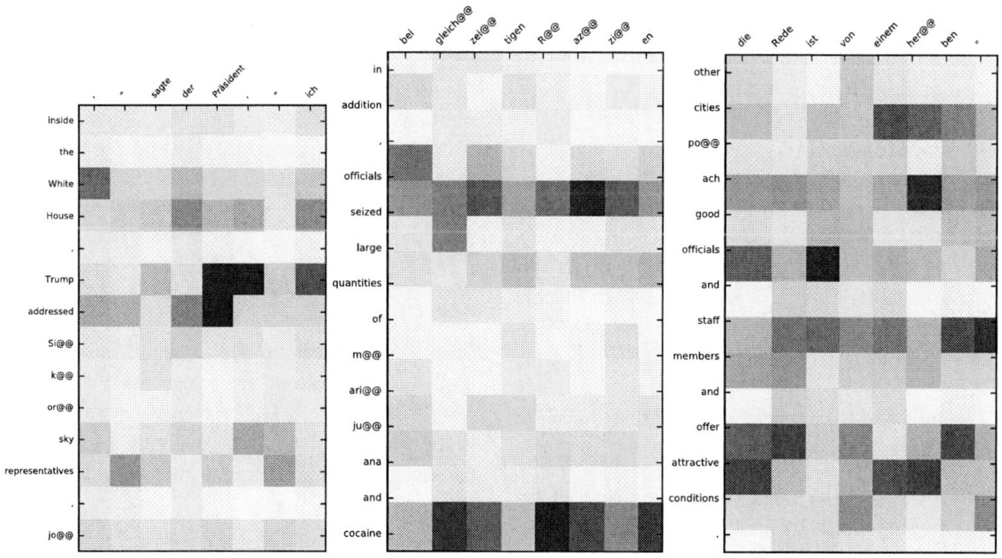

(a) Coreference (b) Topic-aware lexical choice (c) Not interpretable

Figure 7: Attention distribution over context words from target hypothesis.

Condition	System	Bleu [%] en-it	en-de
Dropout 0.1	Sentence-level	31.4	28.9
	Document-level	**32.5**	**30.3**
Dropout 0.3	Sentence-level	**33.7**	**32.3**
	Document-level	33.5	32.0
Large training data	Sentence-level	-	**40.2**
	Document-level	-	39.9

Table 7: Sentence-level vs. document-level translation performance in different data/training conditions.

We argue that the linguistic improvements with document-level NMT have been sometimes oversold, and the document-level components should be tested on top of a well-regularized NMT system. In our experiments, we obtain a much stronger sentence-level baseline by applying a simple regularization (dropout), which the document-level model cannot outperform (Table 7).

On a larger scale, we also built a sentence-level model with all parallel training data available for the WMT 2019 task and fine-tuned only with document-level data (Europarl, News Commentary, newstest2008-2014/2016). The document-level training does not give any improvement in Bleu (last two rows of Table 7). There may exist document-level improvements which are not highlighted by the automatic metrics, but the amount of such improvements must be very small without a clear gain in Bleu or Ter.

5 Conclusion

In this work, we critically investigate the advantages of document-level NMT with a thorough qualitative analysis and expose the limit of its improvements in terms of context length and model complexity. Regarding the questions asked in Section 1, our answers are:

- In general, document-level context is utilized rarely in an interpretable way.
- We conjecture that a dominant cause of the improvements by document-level NMT is actually the regularization of the model.
- Not all of the words in the context are used in the model; we leave out redundant tokens without loss of performance.
- A long-range context gives only marginal additional improvements.
- Word embeddings are sufficient to model document-level context.

For a fair evaluation of document-level NMT methods, we argue that one should make a sentence-level NMT baseline as strong as possible first, i.e. by using more data or applying proper regularization. This will get rid of by-product improvements from additional information flows and help to focus only on document-level errors in translation. In this condition, we show that document-level NMT can barely improve translation metric scores against such strong baselines. Targeted test sets (Bawden et al., 2018; Voita et al., 2019) might be helpful here to emphasize the document-level improvements. However, one should bear in mind that a big improvement in such test sets may not carry over to practical scenarios with general test sets, where the number of document-level errors in translation is inherently small.

Given these conclusions, a future research direction would be building a lightweight post-editing model to correct only document-level errors, not complicating the sentence-level model too much for a very limited amount of document-level improvements. To strengthen our arguments, we also plan to conduct the same qualitative analysis on other types of context inputs (e.g. translation history) and different domains.

Our implementation of document-level NMT methods is publicly available on the web.[6]

Acknowledgments

This work has received funding from the European Research Council (ERC) (under the European Union's Horizon 2020 research and innovation programme, grant agreement No 694537, project "SEQCLAS"). The work reflects only the authors' views and none of the funding agencies is responsible for any use that may be made of the information it contains.

The authors thank Tina Raissi for analyzing English→Italian translations.

[6]https://github.com/ducthanhtran/sockeye_document_context

References

Ruchit Rajeshkumar Agrawal, Marco Turchi, and Matteo Negri. 2018. Contextual handling in neural machine translation: Look behind, ahead and on both sides. In *21st Annual Conference of the European Association for Machine Translation*, pages 11–20.

Alan Akbik, Duncan Blythe, and Roland Vollgraf. 2018. Contextual string embeddings for sequence labeling. In *Proceedings of the 27th International Conference on Computational Linguistics, COLING 2018, Santa Fe, New Mexico, USA, August 20-26, 2018*, pages 1638–1649.

Dzmitry Bahdanau, Kyunghyun Cho, and Yoshua Bengio. 2015. Neural machine translation by jointly learning to align and translate. In *3rd International Conference on Learning Representations, ICLR 2015, San Diego, CA, USA, May 7-9, 2015, Conference Track Proceedings.*

Rachel Bawden, Rico Sennrich, Alexandra Birch, and Barry Haddow. 2018. Evaluating discourse phenomena in neural machine translation. In *Proceedings of the 2018 Conference of the North American Chapter of the Association for Computational Linguistics: Human Language Technologies, Volume 1 (Long Papers)*, pages 1304–1313.

Qian Cao and Deyi Xiong. 2018. Encoding gated translation memory into neural machine translation. In *Proceedings of the 2018 Conference on Empirical Methods in Natural Language Processing*, pages 3042–3047.

Annette Rios Gonzales, Laura Mascarell, and Rico Sennrich. 2017. Improving word sense disambiguation in neural machine translation with sense embeddings. In *Proceedings of the Second Conference on Machine Translation*, pages 11–19.

Liane Guillou, Christian Hardmeier, Ekaterina Lapshinova-Koltunski, and Sharid Loáiciga. 2018. A pronoun test suite evaluation of the english–german mt systems at wmt 2018. In *Proceedings of the Third Conference on Machine Translation: Shared Task Papers*, pages 570–577.

Felix Hieber, Tobias Domhan, Michael Denkowski, David Vilar, Artem Sokolov, Ann Clifton, and Matt Post. 2018. The sockeye neural machine translation toolkit at AMTA 2018. In *Proceedings of the 13th Conference of the Association for Machine Translation in the Americas, AMTA 2018, Boston, MA, USA, March 17-21, 2018 - Volume 1: Research Papers*, pages 200–207.

Sebastien Jean, Stanislas Lauly, Orhan Firat, and Kyunghyun Cho. 2017. Does neural machine translation benefit from larger context? *arXiv preprint arXiv:1704.05135.*

Marcin Junczys-Dowmunt. 2019. Microsoft translator at wmt 2019: Towards large-scale document-level neural machine translation. In *Proceedings of the Fourth Conference on Machine Translation (WMT), Volume 2: Shared Task Papers*, pages 424–432, Florence, Italy.

Diederik P. Kingma and Jimmy Ba. 2015. Adam: A method for stochastic optimization. In *3rd International Conference on Learning Representations, ICLR 2015, San Diego, CA, USA, May 7-9, 2015, Conference Track Proceedings.*

Philipp Koehn and Rebecca Knowles. 2017. Six challenges for neural machine translation. In *Proceedings of the First Workshop on Neural Machine Translation*, pages 28–39.

Shaohui Kuang and Deyi Xiong. 2018. Fusing recency into neural machine translation with an intersentence gate model. In *Proceedings of the 27th International Conference on Computational Linguistics*, pages 607–617.

Shaohui Kuang, Deyi Xiong, Weihua Luo, and Guodong Zhou. 2018. Modeling coherence for neural machine translation with dynamic and topic caches. In *Proceedings of the 27th International Conference on Computational Linguistics*, pages 596–606.

Samuel Läubli, Rico Sennrich, and Martin Volk. 2018. Has machine translation achieved human parity? a case for document-level evaluation. In *Proceedings of the 2018 Conference on Empirical Methods in Natural Language Processing*, pages 4791–4796.

Sameen Maruf and Gholamreza Haffari. 2018. Document context neural machine translation with memory networks. In *Proceedings of the 56th Annual Meeting of the Association for Computational Linguistics (Volume 1: Long Papers)*, pages 1275–1284.

Sameen Maruf, André FT Martins, and Gholamreza Haffari. 2019. Selective attention for context-aware neural machine translation. In *Proceedings of the 2019 Conference of the North American Chapter of the Association for Computational Linguistics: Human Language Technologies, Volume 1 (Long and Short Papers)*, pages 3092–3102.

Rebecca Marvin and Philipp Koehn. 2018. Exploring word sense disambiguation abilities of neural machine translation systems (non-archival extended abstract). In *Proceedings of the 13th Conference of the Association for Machine Translation in the Americas (Volume 1: Research Papers)*, pages 125–131.

Lesly Miculicich, Dhananjay Ram, Nikolaos Pappas, and James Henderson. 2018. Document-level neural machine translation with hierarchical attention networks. In *Proceedings of the 2018 Conference on Empirical Methods in Natural Language Processing*, pages 2947–2954.

Xiao Pu, Nikolaos Pappas, James Henderson, and Andrei Popescu-Belis. 2018. Integrating weakly supervised word sense disambiguation into neural machine translation. *Transactions of the Association for Computational Linguistics*, 6:635–649.

Rico Sennrich, Barry Haddow, and Alexandra Birch. 2016. Neural machine translation of rare words with subword units. In *Proceedings of the 54th Annual Meeting of the Association for Computational Linguistics (Volume 1: Long Papers)*, volume 1, pages 1715–1725.

Dario Stojanovski and Alexander Fraser. 2018. Coreference and coherence in neural machine translation: A study using oracle experiments. In *Proceedings of the Third Conference on Machine Translation: Research Papers*, pages 49–60.

Sainbayar Sukhbaatar, Edouard Grave, Piotr Bojanowski, and Armand Joulin. 2019. Adaptive attention span in transformers. In *Proceedings of the 57th Annual Meeting of the Association for Computational Linguistics*, Florence, Italy.

Jörg Tiedemann and Yves Scherrer. 2017. Neural machine translation with extended context. In *Proceedings of the Third Workshop on Discourse in Machine Translation*, pages 82–92.

Zhaopeng Tu, Yang Liu, Shuming Shi, and Tong Zhang. 2018. Learning to remember translation history with a continuous cache. *Transactions of the Association for Computational Linguistics*, 6:407–420.

Ashish Vaswani, Noam Shazeer, Niki Parmar, Jakob Uszkoreit, Llion Jones, Aidan N. Gomez, Lukasz Kaiser, and Illia Polosukhin. 2017. Attention is all you need. In *Advances in Neural Information Processing Systems 30: Annual Conference on Neural Information Processing Systems 2017, 4-9 December 2017, Long Beach, CA, USA*, pages 5998–6008.

Elena Voita, Rico Sennrich, and Ivan Titov. 2019. When a good translation is wrong in context: Context-aware machine translation improves on deixis, ellipsis, and lexical cohesion. In *Proceedings of the 57th Annual Meeting of the Association for Computational Linguistics (ACL 2019)*, pages 1198–1212, Florence, Italy.

Elena Voita, Pavel Serdyukov, Rico Sennrich, and Ivan Titov. 2018. Context-aware neural machine translation learns anaphora resolution. In *Proceedings of the 56th Annual Meeting of the Association for Computational Linguistics (Volume 1: Long Papers)*, pages 1264–1274.

Jiacheng Zhang, Huanbo Luan, Maosong Sun, Feifei Zhai, Jingfang Xu, Min Zhang, and Yang Liu. 2018. Improving the transformer translation model with document-level context. In *Proceedings of the 2018 Conference on Empirical Methods in Natural Language Processing*, pages 533–542.

Data Augmentation using Back-translation for Context-aware Neural Machine Translation

Amane Sugiyama
The University of Tokyo
sugi@tkl.iis.u-tokyo.ac.jp

Naoki Yoshinaga
Institute of Industrial Science,
the University of Tokyo
ynaga@iis.u-tokyo.ac.jp

Abstract

A single sentence does not always convey information required to translate it into other languages; we sometimes need to add or specialize words that are omitted or ambiguous in the source languages (*e.g.*, zero pronouns in translating Japanese to English or epicene pronouns in translating English to French). To translate such ambiguous sentences, we exploit contexts around the source sentence, and have so far explored context-aware neural machine translation (NMT). However, a large amount of parallel corpora is not easily available to train accurate context-aware NMT models. In this study, we first obtain large-scale pseudo parallel corpora by back-translating target-side monolingual corpora, and then investigate its impact on the translation performance of context-aware NMT models. We evaluate NMT models trained with small parallel corpora and the large-scale pseudo parallel corpora on IWSLT2017 English-Japanese and English-French datasets, and demonstrate the large impact of the data augmentation for context-aware NMT models in terms of BLEU score and specialized test sets on ja→en[1] and fr→en.

1 Introduction

Following the success of neural machine translation (NMT) models in sentence-level translation, context-aware NMT models have been studied to further boost the quality of translation (Jean et al., 2017; Tiedemann and Scherrer, 2017; Wang et al., 2017; Bawden et al., 2018; Voita et al., 2018; Maruf and Haffari, 2018; Miculicich et al., 2018; Maruf et al., 2019; Voita et al., 2019). These context-aware models take auxiliary inputs (contexts) to translate the source sentence which lacks information needed for translating into the target language (§ 2). Typically, contexts considered by context-aware NMT are surrounding sentences in the same document (Tiedemann and Scherrer, 2017; Bawden et al., 2018; Voita et al., 2018; Maruf and Haffari, 2018; Voita et al., 2019), which provide beneficial information in translating zero pronouns, anaphoric pronouns, lexically ambiguous words, and so on.

[1] http://www.tkl.iis.u-tokyo.ac.jp/~sugi/DiscoMT2019/

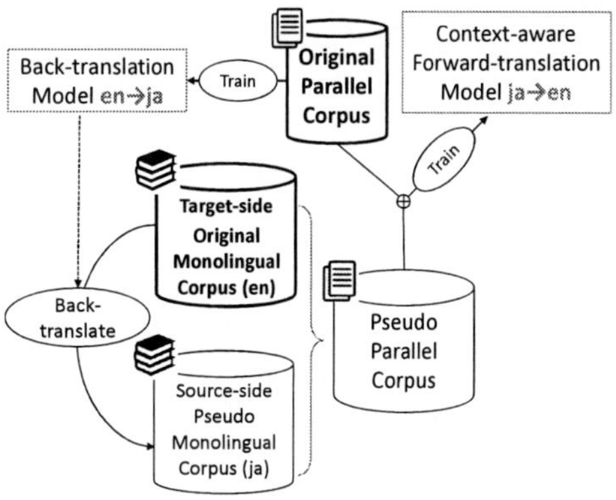

Figure 1: Overview of the data augmentation for context-aware NMT (Japanese to English in this case).

Although the context-aware NMT models outperform the baseline sentence-level NMT models in terms of BLEU score and some specialized test sets (Bawden et al., 2018; Voita et al., 2019; Müller et al., 2018), the reported gains, especially in BLEU score, are often marginal. We can think of several reasons for this; 1) the ratio of sentences (or linguistic phenomena) that require contexts for translation is small in the evaluation datasets, 2) the current context-aware models do not fully utilize the given contexts, 3) (narrow) contexts considered in context-aware NMT models do not include information required for translation, 4) the size of training data is not enough to effectively train context-aware NMT models. Although there are some studies that investigate the first to third

Proceedings of the Fourth Workshop on Discourse in Machine Translation (DiscoMT 2019), pages 35–44
Hong Kong, China, November 3, 2019.

aspects (Bawden et al., 2018; Voita et al., 2018; Imamura and Sumita, 2019), few studies have investigated the last possibility (§ 6), since there are few parallel corpora for context-aware translation; existing large-scale and high-quality parallel corpora are usually obtained by extracting reliable sentence alignments from translations by humans (Nakazawa et al., 2016; Pryzant et al., 2018). Considering that context-aware NMT models have larger input spaces than sentence-level models, they will demand larger training data to fully exert the models' performance.

In this study, we hypothesize that context-aware NMT models can benefit from an increase of the training data more than sentence-level models, and confirm this by performing data augmentation using back-translation (Sennrich et al., 2016b) (§ 6) for context-aware NMT models. We propose to assist the training of context-aware NMT models using pseudo parallel data which is automatically generated by back-translating a large monolingual data (§ 3, Figure 1). The back-translation model here is trained on an existing parallel corpus. Since context-aware models are designed to recover information that is absent from the source sentence but should be present in the target sentence, back-translation can produce effective training data if it could naturally drop the information to be recovered in translating sentences in the target language into the source language.

We evaluate our method on IWSLT2017 data sets (Cettolo et al., 2012), which are collections of subtitles of TED Talks, on two language pairs: English-Japanese (en-ja) and English-French (en-fr) (§ 4). We exploit BookCorpus (Zhu et al., 2015), Europarl v7 (Koehn, 2005), and the record of the National Diet of Japan as monolingual corpora for back-translation (§ 5). Experimental results revealed that the data augmentation improved the translation in terms of BLEU score (Papineni et al., 2002) and the accuracy on specialized test sets for context-aware NMT.

The contribution of this paper is as follows:

- We **first evaluated data augmentation on context-aware NMT**, and confirmed BLEU improvement on en↔fr and ja→en datasets,
- **developed a new specialized test set for evaluating ja→en** context-aware translation, and
- **confirmed that the data augmentation improves context-aware translation** through the existing en→fr (Bawden et al., 2018) and our specialized test set for ja→en translation.

2 Context-aware NMT Models

To incorporate contexts to translate sentences, recent studies on NMT have explored context-aware models which take sentences around the source sentence as auxiliary inputs. Typical contexts considered in those models are a few sentences that precede the source sentence.

The context-aware NMT models are grouped into two types: single-encoder models that apply a sentence-level NMT model to the source sentence concatenated after their contexts (preceding sentence(s)) (Tiedemann and Scherrer, 2017; Bawden et al., 2018) and multi-encoder models that design an additional context encoder to process the contexts (Jean et al., 2017; Wang et al., 2017; Bawden et al., 2018; Voita et al., 2018; Maruf and Haffari, 2018; Miculicich et al., 2018; Tu et al., 2018; Maruf et al., 2019). In what follows, we briefly review these models.

Single-encoder models take the preceding sentence(s) as the contexts in addition to the source sentence and concatenate them with a special symbol <CONC> (Tiedemann and Scherrer, 2017). The concatenated sentences are then translated using an existing sentence-level NMT model.

There are two subtypes of the single-encoder models that differ in handling contexts in the target language. The first model, which we refer to as 2-to-1, only considers contexts in the source language, and is trained on pairs of the source sentence with the preceding sentence(s) and the target sentence. It learns a mapping from the source sentence with its context to the target sentence. The second one, which we refer to as 2-to-2, considers contexts in both the source and target languages. 2-to-2 models are trained on pairs of the source sentence with the preceding sentence(s) and the target sentence with the preceding sentence(s). At test time of a 2-to-2 model, the decoder receives the encoder hidden states and the translation of the previous sentence, which has been generated in the previous translation step. We analogically refer to the standard sentence-level NMT models as 1-to-1 to highlight the difference in input and output.

Multi-encoder models take the preceding sentence(s) as the contexts, and use additional neural networks to encode the contexts. Several network architectures have been explored for this additional encoder (Jean et al., 2017; Wang et al., 2017; Bawden et al., 2018; Voita et al., 2018; Maruf and Haffari, 2018; Miculicich et al., 2018; Tu et al., 2018).

In this study, we adopt the standard single-encoder model (Tiedemann and Scherrer, 2017) in our experiments (§ 4), since both single-encoder and multi-encoder models are reported to outperform the sentence-level models and the performance gap between the two context-aware models are marginal. We then focus on investigating the impact of additional pseudo parallel training data generated by back-translation. Note that the single-encoder models are simpler, and we can employ the well-established NMT architectures such as Transformer (Vaswani et al., 2017) without any modifications for sequence-to-sequence transformation.

3 Data Augmentation for Context-aware NMT using Back-translation

We hypothesize that context-aware NMT models can benefit from an increase of the training data more than sentence-level NMT models, and experimentally confirm this by training and evaluating context-aware NMT models with additional training data. We propose to use data augmentation based on back-translation (Sennrich et al., 2016a) to obtain the additional training data for context-aware NMT models. We hereafter refer to (final) source-to-target translation as *forward-translation* to distinguish it with (target-to-source) back-translation for data augmentation.

The pseudo parallel data is automatically generated by back-translating large target-side monolingual corpora (target→source). Since monolingual corpora can be obtained more easily than bilingual parallel corpora which are aligned at sentence level, the back-translation allows us to train a context-aware NMT model with larger data. We can expect the resulting pseudo parallel corpora to contain more cases from which the model can learn to use contexts in translation.

Back-translation for data augmentation The data augmentation in this study follows the existing back-translation strategies for NMT (Sennrich et al., 2016a; Imamura et al., 2018; Edunov et al., 2018) except that we assume a context-aware model for the forward-translation; the monolingual data for back-translation must be a set of documents each of which consists of contiguous sentences. This data-augmentation approach would naturally benefit context-aware models more than sentence-level models because the former are to handle a larger input/output space, which makes them more complex as a mapping task.

Here, we describe our training process to obtain pseudo training data for translation from the source (L_S) to the target (L_T) language.

Train a back-translation model ($L_T \rightarrow L_S$)
Given a (small) parallel data for source language L_S and target language L_T, we first train a back-translation model $L_T \rightarrow L_S$ on the parallel data.

Back-translate L_T monolingual data into L_S
We next back-translate a large L_T (target-side) monolingual data to generate pseudo L_S (source-side) monolingual data, which forms pseudo parallel data together with the original target-side monolingual data. Note that sentential alignments are naturally obtained through the translation.

Train a forward-translation model ($L_S \rightarrow L_T$)
We then train the forward-translation model from the original parallel data augmented with the obtained pseudo parallel data.

The pseudo parallel data has merits and demerits against human-translated parallel data which is automatically aligned. The pseudo parallel data is inferior to the human-translated parallel data in that it is generated automatically by a possibly inaccurate machine translation system. However, it does not contain mismatches of sentence boundaries between the target and the obtained (back-translated) source monolingual data, in contrast to the human-translated data where, for example, a source sentence can correspond to multiple target sentences.

On back-translation model We can use either a sentence-level or context-aware NMT model for back-translation. In the following experiments, we first adopt 2-to-1 NMT model as a back-translator for data augmentation, and evaluate the impact of the data augmentation on the translation performance of context-aware NMT models. We then compare those results with results obtained by the data augmentation using 1-to-1 and 2-to-2 models instead of 2-to-1 model for back-translation.

	# sentence pairs	avg. source length	avg. target length
en→ja	223k / 0.87k / 1.54k	24.7 / 28.0 / 24.6	25.4 / 27.9 / 24.5
ja→en	212k / 0.87k / 1.54k	22.3 / 28.0 / 24.6	22.8 / 27.9 / 24.5
en→fr	222k / 0.89k / 1.56k	22.1 / 27.2 / 24.3	23.5 / 28.0 / 25.8
fr→en	222k / 0.89k / 1.56k	23.5 / 28.0 / 25.8	22.1 / 27.2 / 24.3

Table 1: Statistics of IWSLT2017 corpora: the number of sentence pairs and the average length (number of tokens per sentence) for the train / dev / test portions.

We can expect context-aware NMT models to moderately omit redundant information as humans do and to yield more natural translations when back-translating, especially if the source language L_S prefers to omit redundant expressions (*e.g.*, zero pronouns in Japanese). It would produce a better training data from which the forward-translation model can learn to restore the omitted information referring to context.

4 Experimental settings

This section describes experimental settings to evaluate the impact of the data augmentation on context-aware NMT models. We conduct translation experiments on two language pairs for both directions: Japanese→English (hereafter, ja→en), English→Japanese (en→ja), French→English (fr→en), and English→French (en→fr) using publicly available corpora of spoken language that are used in the previous studies.

Datasets (parallel corpora) For all the language pairs, we use IWSLT2017 corpus[2] (Cettolo et al., 2012) as the original (human-translated) parallel data. This corpus is made from subtitles of TED Talks. The English subtitles are transcription of the talks and the subtitles in the other languages are translations of the English subtitles. We consider each talk as a document. We use `dev2010` for development and `tst2010` for evaluation in each language pair. The statistics of IWSLT2017 corpus used in our experiments are listed in Table 1.

Datasets (monolingual corpora) For ja→en and fr→en translations, we exploit BookCorpus (Zhu et al., 2015) as the monolingual data. BookCorpus is a collection of English e-books available on the Web.[3] We extract paragraphs from BookCorpus that consist of more than 9 sentences and treat them as single documents. For en→ja and en→fr translation, we adopt the record of the National Diet of Japan[4] (hereafter, DietCorpus) and Europarl corpus v7[5] (Koehn, 2005) as the monolingual data, respectively. We use the French part of Europarl as a monolingual corpus in our experiments considering its domain being close to that of IWSLT2017 (most documents in Europarl corpus consist of conversation of multiple persons but each block of contiguous utterances given by a single person tends to be long so it can be assumed to be locally monologue like IWSLT2017) and it consists of contiguous sentences, which meets our demand.

Preprocessing We normalize punctuation of the English and French datasets and perform tokenization and truecasing using Moses toolkit verion 4.0.[6] We tokenize the Japanese datasets using MeCab verion 0.996 with ipadic dictionary verion 2.7.0.[7] For each language pair, we finally split datasets into subword units using SentencePiece (verion 0.1.81)[8] with unigram language model. The SentencePiece model is trained using the original parallel corpus (IWSLT2017 corpus) following (Sennrich et al., 2016a; Imamura et al., 2018). The vocabulary size is 16k shared by the source and target languages.

Prior to training, all 1-to-1 back-translation models and 1-to-1 forward-translation models for ja→en and en↔fr, we remove from the training datasets sentence pairs in which the source or target sentence contains more than 64 tokens. We set a larger limit of 128 in training the 1-to-1 forward-translation model of en→ja since the Japanese monolingual corpus DietCorpus has longer sentences on average and the limit of 64 is too small to cover an adequate proportion of sentence pairs

[2] `https://wit3.fbk.eu/mt.php`

[3] We used a crawler available at `https://github.com/soskek/bookcorpus`

[4] `https://www2.ninjal.ac.jp/lrc/index.php`

[5] `https://www.statmt.org/europarl/`

[6] `http://www.statmt.org/moses/`

[7] `https://taku910.github.io/mecab/`

[8] `https://github.com/google/sentencepiece`

	# sentences	avg. source length	avg. target length
en→ja	1030k	31.9	39.7
ja→en	6493k	16.4	14.9
en→fr	2223k	26.8	30.0
fr→en	6493k	16.0	14.9

Table 2: Statistics of the target-side monolingual corpora and their source-side counterparts obtained by back-translation: the number of sentences in the original corpora and the average length in the pseudo parallel data used to train 1-to-1 models.

in the monolingual corpus. Prior to training 2-to-X forward-translation models, we removed pairs of concatenated sentences where the source or target contains more than 128 tokens except en→ja forward-translation with the length limit of 200 for the same reason as above. The statistics of the datasets we used to train 1-to-1 models are shown in Table 1 and 2.[9]

NMT models For all NMT models, we adopted Transformer (Vaswani et al., 2017) as the core neural model architecture. We implemented it using Tensorflow[10] verion 1.12.0. Both encoder and decoder comprise 6 blocks, the dimension of the embedding layers is 512 and the dimension of the FFN layers is 2048. The source and target embedding weights and the decoder pre-softmax weights are all shared. Training is performed using Adam optimizer (Kingma and Ba, 2015) with a learning rate conditioned on the training steps following the original Transformer. Each batch contains about $16384 (= 128^2)$ tokens, and hence the number of sentences in a batch varies.

Back-translation For each language pair, back-translation models are trained on IWSLT2017 corpora. Monolingual data are back-translated by using 2-to-1 models with beam size of 5.

Forward-translation For each language pair, we train 1-to-1, 2-to-1 and 2-to-2 models while varying the size of pseudo parallel data used to augment the original parallel data. We train ja→en and fr→en models on 0k (none), 500k, 1000k, 2000k and 4000k pseudo data, en→ja models on 0k (none), 500k and 1000k pseudo data, and en→fr models on 0k (none), 500k, 1000k and 2000k pseudo data. At test time, we perform translation with beam size of 8.

Evaluation using BLEU We evaluate the translation quality of the forward-translation with BLEU scores (Papineni et al., 2002), computed by `multi-bleu.perl` in the Moses toolkit, after decoding the subwords by SentencePiece.

Evaluation using specialized test sets Also, we perform evaluation on en→fr and ja→en translation using an existing (Bawden et al., 2018) and a newly-created specialized test sets for evaluating context-aware NMT. These datasets are designed to assess whether NMT models capture intersentential contexts.

Both test sets consist of questions to be asked to the model. In each question, given a source sentence, source-side context, target-side context and two translation candidates, models must determine which one of the two candidates is correct as a translation for the source sentence on the basis of the translation scores (in our experiments, we compute translation scores from log-likelihood of the sequences with length-normalization (Johnson et al., 2017)). Both test sets are designed so that sentence-level models always achieve 50% accuracy.

For en→fr 2-to-2 models,[11] we exploit the existing discourse test sets tailored by Bawden et al. (2018). The test set include coreference test set and coherence/cohesion test set. The coreference test set contains 200 questions, which require NMT models to implicitly resolve anaphora to translate anaphoric pronouns. The coherence/cohesion test set contains 200 questions to test how well NMT models maintain discourse-level consistency. Note that this dataset was made on the basis of OpenSubtitles2016 corpus (Lison and Tiedemann, 2016), and, in some questions, the context and the main sentence form a dialogue; the domain does not fully match that of our parallel corpus (TED talks, monologue).

For ja→en models, following (Bawden et al., 2018), we newly created a specialized test set. Referring to (Nagata and Morishita, 2019), we tailored test cases focusing on zero pronouns in Japanese for the specialized test set as follows.[12] First, we choose two contiguous sentences, as the

[9]Training of 2-to-X models is done using different subsets of the whole pseudo parallel data (due to the different cleaning standards stated in this paragraph). Since the statistics of the pseudo parallel data are almost identical, we provide here the statistics of 1-to-1 as representative.

[10]`https://www.tensorflow.org/`

[11]We only evaluate 2-to-2 models because some questions in the datasets require target-side contexts to answer.

[12]We developed a new ja→en test set since Nagata and Morishita (2019) does not release their test set.

# pseudo train (# sent. pairs)	en→ja / # train: 212k			ja→en / # train: 211k			en→fr / # train: 222k			fr→en / # train: 222k		
	1-to-1	2-to-1	2-to-2	1-to-1	2-to-1	2-to-2	1-to-1	2-to-1	2-to-2	1-to-1	2-to-1	2-to-2
0k	**12.47**	**12.88**	12.42	11.07	11.32	11.76	36.77	36.83	37.03	35.73	36.16	36.29
500k	12.32	12.79	**12.54**	11.92	12.68	13.04	38.08	38.05	38.16	37.22	37.07	37.37
1000k	11.98	11.99	12.28	12.03	12.80	13.20	**38.11**	37.63	38.55	37.11	37.20	37.90
2000k	n/a	n/a	n/a	11.84	12.91	**13.57**	37.98	**38.30**	**38.79**	37.36	**37.86**	37.86
4000k	n/a	n/a	n/a	**12.14**	**13.06**	13.51	n/a	n/a	n/a	**37.47**	37.44	**38.01**

Table 3: BLEU scores of the sentence-level and context-aware models with data augmentation: All the models are trained on the original parallel corpora and the pseudo parallel data generated by back-translation, while varying the size of pseudo training data from 0 (no pseudo training data) to 4000k.

Source
context: 父親 は 何 か 呟い て い た 。
sentece: どうも ドア の ほう に 向き なおっ て いる らしい 。
Target
context: My **father** murmured something.
correct: He seems to be turning towards the door.
incorrect: She seems to be turning towards the door.

Source
context: 母親 は 何 か 呟い て い た 。
sentence: どうも ドア の ほう に 向き なおっ て いる らしい 。
Target
context: My **mother** murmured something.
correct: She seems to be turning towards the door.
incorrect: He seems to be turning towards the door.

Figure 2: An example pair of questions in our ja→en test set; the underlined pronouns refer to the boldfaced nouns, and do not appear in the source Japanese sentences (zero pronouns).

source sentence and its context, denoted by S and C_{s_1} respectively, from a Japanese corpus, Keyaki Treebank (Butler et al., 2018), and translate them into English, which result in a correct translation and the target-side context, denoted by T_1 and C_{t_1}, respectively. Next, we write an incorrect translation T_2 and source/target contexts C_{s_2}, C_{t_2} with which the incorrect translation could be correct. Then, using these sentences, we make two questions:

Q_1: given $S, C_{s_1}, C_{t_1}, T_1, T_2$, choose T_1 or T_2

Q_2: given $S, C_{s_2}, C_{t_2}, T_1, T_2$, choose T_1 or T_2

For Q_1 and Q_2, the correct answer is T_1 and T_2, respectively. By iterating this process, we made 100 questions. Note that sentence-level models achieve exactly 50% accuracy on this test set. Unlike the en→fr test set, all the questions are answerable without seeing the target-side context. Some of the created questions are shown in Figure 2.

5 Results and Analysis

In this section, we first report the impact of the data augmentation on sentence-level and context-aware NMTs (§ 5.1). We next investigate whether the translation performance with the data augmentation is affected by the type of translation system used for back-translation: single-sentence NMT or context-aware NMT (§ 5.2). We then confirm that the data augmentation improves ja→en and en→fr translation that requires contexts by using the two discourse-oriented test sets (§ 5.3). We finally show some translation examples (§ 5.4).

5.1 Impact of the size of pseudo training data

Table 3 lists the BLEU scores of sentence-level and context-aware NMT models while varying the size of pseudo parallel data. In what follows, we interpret results in detail.

ja→en and en↔fr models A comparison among 1-to-1, 2-to-1, and 2-to2 models provides a certain trend; context-aware models (2-to-X) are better than the sentence-level model (1-to-1), and the target-side contexts contribute to the translation quality (2-to-1 vs. 2-to-2). The impact of the pseudo parallel data is clear: adding pseudo parallel data to a certain extent results in higher BLEU scores; 2-to-X models achieve the best performance with more pseudo data than 1-to-1 models. In other words, context-aware models with auxiliary inputs benefit from more pseudo parallel data, as we have expected; 2-to-2 models benefit from the largest pseudo training data.

We additively obtained the gain in BLEU by using the pseudo parallel data in addition to using contexts. This results in a large improvement in BLEU scores: +2.50 (11.07 → 13.57) in ja→en, +2.02 (36.77 → 38.79) in en→fr, and then +2.28 (35.73 → 38.01) in fr→en.

	pseudo train	train	dev	test
en	14 / 27 / 45	13 / 20 / 32	14 / 23 / 35	13 / 20 / 31
ja	18 / 34 / 56	13 / 21 / 33	13 / 22 / 37	12 / 20 / 32

Table 4: The quartile of the number of tokens per sentence in each dataset: train, dev and test indicate the train, dev, and test sets of IWSLT2017 corpus. The English portion of the pseudo train dataset is the translation of the Japanese monolingual corpus, DietCorpus.

# pseudo	1-to-1 back-trans.			2-to-1 back-trans.			2-to-2 back-trans.		
train	1-to-1	2-to-1	2-to-2	1-to-1	2-to-1	2-to-2	1-to-1	2-to-1	2-to-2
0k	11.07	11.32	11.76	(same to the left)					
500k	12.02	12.90	13.02	11.92	12.68	13.04	12.15	12.65	13.35
1000k	12.41	12.99	13.22	12.03	12.80	13.20	12.43	13.19	13.49
2000k	**12.49**	**13.35**	**13.57**	11.84	12.91	**13.57**	12.59	13.40	**13.79**
4000k	12.23	13.02	13.34	**12.14**	**13.06**	13.51	**12.78**	**13.34**	13.58

Table 5: The BLEU scores of ja→en context-aware models trained with pseudo parallel data generated by 1-to-1 and 2-to-2 back-translation: The scores of the models trained on pseudo data generated by 2-to-1 back-translation are excerpted from Table 3.

en→ja models The additional data did not contribute to the translation quality, which indicates that the data augmentation using back-translation was not effective. This is partly due to difficult ja→en (back-)translation, and partly due to the difference between the original and pseudo parallel corpora. As shown in Table 4, there is clearly a gap between the original and pseudo parallel corpora in terms of the number of tokens per sentence. In IWSLT2017 datasets, the average number of tokens per sentence is almost equivalent between English and Japanese while in the pseudo parallel data English sentences are significantly shorter than the Japanese counterparts. This implies that some information has been lost in back-translating the Japanese monolingual corpus into English, and thus mismatches of the contents of the sentences in the two languages are likely to occur.

5.2 1-to-1 vs. 2-to-1 back-translation

To confirm the effect of using context-aware models instead of sentence-level models for back-translation, we additionally train ja→en models using pseudo parallel data generated by 1-to-1 and 2-to-2 back-translation. We train 1-to-1, 2-to-1, and 2-to-2 models on 500k, 1000k, 2000 and 4000k pseudo data. We conduct an evaluation using BLEU and the specialized test set we created (reported later in § 5.3), and compare the results with those trained on pseudo data generated by 2-to-1 back-translation.

Table 5 shows the evaluation results in BLEU. We observe comparable effect of the two back-translation methods, 1-to-1 and 2-to-1, on the forward-translation, whereas the 2-to-2 back-translation results in slightly higher scores of the forward-translation over the other two methods.

		Coref.	Coherence /cohesion
Bawden et al. (2018) / # train: 29M			
2-TO-2 (single-encoder best)		63.5	52.0
S-HIER-TO-2 (multi-encoder best)		72.5	**57.0**
2-to-2 (this paper)	/ # train: 222k		
(# pseudo train)	0k	70.0	51.0
	500k	76.5	51.5
	1000k	78.0	52.5
	2000k	**78.5**	52.5

Table 6: Results of 2-to-2 models on the en→fr specialized test sets (accuracy in %).

# pseudo	1-to-1 back-t.		2-to-1 back-t.		2-to-2 back-t.	
train	2-to-1	2-to-2	2-to-1	2-to-2	2-to-1	2-to-2
0k	78	79	(same to the left)			
500k	87	84	85	89	83	89
1000k	**91**	89	81	89	**88**	88
2000k	86	90	88	**93**	87	**90**
4000k	85	**93**	**91**	**93**	86	89

Table 7: Results of 2-to-X models on the ja→en specialized test sets (accuracy in %).

5.3 Evaluation of context-aware translation using specialized test sets

Table 6 and 7 show results on the en→fr and ja→en specialized test sets, respectively. In what follows, we interpret results in detail.

Source	
context	彼女$_1$ の 20 代 も 困難 な もの でし た が Φ_2 それ 以前 の 人生 は もっと 困難 に 溢れ て い まし た
sentence	Φ_3 診察 中 何 度 も 涙 を 流し まし た が 「 家族 は 選べ ない けど 友達 は 選べ る 」 と その たび に 言っ て 気持ち を 落ち着か せ て い まし た
Target	
context	and as hard as **her**$_1$ 20s were , **her**$_2$ early life had been even harder .
sentence	**she**$_3$ often cried in our sessions, but then would collect herself by saying, "you can't pick your family, but you can pick your friends."
1-to-1	**I**'ve had tears in my doctor's office, and **I**'ve said, "I don't have a family, but I've got a friend," and **I** calmed down every time.
1-to-1 +2M pseudo data	**I** cried a lot during my examination, but every time **I** said, "I can't choose a family, but I can choose a friend," **I** said calmly.
2-to-2	during **my** diagnosis, **I** ran a lot of tears, and **I** said, "no family can choose," but every time I said, "I can choose a friend," **I** kind of calmed down.
2-to-2 +2M pseudo data	**she** cried many times during her examination, but each time she said, "I can't choose a family, but I can choose a friend," **she** said calmly.

Table 8: Example of translated sentences; zero pronoun Φ_3 is successfully restored in by the 2-to-2 model trained using 2M pseudo data. The corresponding pronouns in the source and target are modified with the same subscripts.

en→fr models Table 6 shows the results of 2-to-2 models with the data augmentation and the best performing models excerpted from (Bawden et al., 2018). 2-TO-2 is a single-encoder model using seq2seq (Bahdanau et al., 2015) instead of Transformer we have adopted, while S-HIER-TO-2 is a multi-encoder model. These models are trained from OpenSubtitles2016 corpus, which has 29M sentence pairs in the same domain as the test set.

When trained on a larger pseudo parallel data, 2-to-2 models achieved a higher accuracy for both coreference and coherence/cohesion datasets. Our 2-to-2 model trained using 2M pseudo parallel data outperforms by 15.0% and 6.0% on the coreference test set against the best-performing single and multi-encoder models trained with 29M in-domain parallel data. A possible explanation for this is that the coreference test is less domain-specific compared to the coherence/cohesion test set. To answer a typical question in the coreference test set, models need to recognize the pronouns in the source sentence, next find the antecedents of them in the source/target contexts, and then check if the gender agrees between them. This process, in most cases, does not require deep knowledge of the antecedent words because gender of a French word tends to be identified by its surface or the article and adjectives attached to it. On the other hand, the coherence/cohesion test includes questions imposing domain-specific tasks like lexical disambiguation, which require more knowledge about particular words specific to the domain. This explains the limited accuracy of our models trained in the domain of IWSLT2017 and Europarl, in contrast to the multi-encoder model S-HIER-TO-2 which is trained on OpenSubtitles2016, the same domain as the test set, achieving larger improvement.

ja→en models Table 7 lists the results of context-aware models. The models trained with larger pseudo parallel data achieve higher accuracy, as we have observed in the en→fr test set.

5.4 Qualitative Analysis

Table 8 shows examples of ja→en translation where the use of contexts and additional pseudo training data help improve the translation quality. Adding 2M pseudo data for training to the 1-to-1 model makes the translation much more fluent although the model cannot restore the correct pronoun "she." On the other hand, 2-to-2 without additional data cannot restore the correct pronoun either, and its translation is as awkward as that of the 1-to-1 model. By extending the sentence-level model with contexts (from both source and target) and adding pseudo data (2-to-2 + 2M pseudo training data), we obtain the best translation.

6 Related Work

Sennrich et al. (2016a) introduce a basic framework to exploit monolingual data (data augmentation by back-translation) for NMT. Imamura et al. (2018) show that back-translation using sampling instead of beam search generates more diverse synthetic source sentences which are effective for enhancing the encoder. Edunov et al. (2018) further investigate the optimal back-translation procedure by comparing several methods such as beam search, random sampling and adding filter noise that randomly masks words in the synthetic source sentences. They focus on back-translation for sentence-level NMT whereas our interest lies in back-translation for context-aware models.

Although we have used simple beam search with the beam size of 5 for back-translation, those randomized back-translation strategies, if adopted, should strongly boost our baseline (sentence-level translation), as reported in (Imamura et al., 2018). These strategies can be applicable to the data augmentation for context-aware NMT, and would also improve the context-aware models' ability to capture contexts because they, especially adding filler noise (Edunov et al., 2018), produce source/target pairs in which some useful information for disambiguation is lost and the models need to try to find alternative hints in the context.

7 Conclusions

In this study, based on our hypothesis that the performance of context-aware models is more affected by the lack of the training data than sentence-level NMT models, we investigated the impact of large-scale parallel data on the translation quality of context-aware models. We conduct experiments of data augmentation based on back-translation, on four language directions en→ja, ja→en, en→fr and fr→en using IWSLT2017 datasets. The results of BLEU evaluation for ja→en and en→fr support our hypothesis. Through evaluation using the existing en→fr test set and our new ja→en test set, which are specialized in evaluating context-aware NMT models, we demonstrate that pseudo parallel data enhance context-aware NMT models in terms of the ability to capture contextual information.

In the future, we plan to assess the effectiveness of our approach on stronger baselines: multi-encoder models and the randomized back-translation strategies.

Acknowledgments

We deeply thank Dr. Shonosuke Ishiwatari for giving valuable comments on the early draft of this paper. This work was supported by JST CREST Grant Number JPMJCR19A4, Japan.

References

Dzmitry Bahdanau, Kyunghyun Cho, and Yoshua Bengio. 2015. Neural machine translation by jointly learning to align and translate. In *Proceedings of the third International Conference on Learning Representations (ICLR)*.

Rachel Bawden, Rico Sennrich, Alexandra Birch, and Barry Haddow. 2018. Evaluating discourse phenomena in neural machine translation. In *Proceedings of the 2018 Conference of the North American Chapter of the Association for Computational Linguistics: Human Language Technologies (NAACL-HLT)*, pages 1304–1313.

Alastair Butler, Kei Yoshimoto, Shota Hiyama, Stephen Wright Horn, Iku Nagasaki, and Ai Kubota. 2018. The keyaki treebank parsed corpus, version 1.1. `http://www.compling.jp/keyaki/` accessed on 2019/06/01.

Mauro Cettolo, Christian Girardi, and Marcello Federico. 2012. Wit3: Web inventory of transcribed and translated talks. In *Proceedings of the 16th Annual Conference of European Association for Machine Translation (EAMT)*, pages 261–268.

Sergey Edunov, Myle Ott, Michael Auli, and David Grangier. 2018. Understanding back-translation at scale. In *Proceedings of the 2018 Conference on Empirical Methods in Natural Language Processing (EMNLP)*, pages 489–500.

Kenji Imamura, Atsushi Fujita, and Eiichiro Sumita. 2018. Enhancement of encoder and attention using target monolingual corpora in neural machine translation. In *Proceedings of the Second Workshop on Neural Machine Translation and Generation (WNMT)*, pages 55–63.

Kenji Imamura and Eiichiro Sumita. 2019. Incorporating long-distance contexts into dialogue translation. In *Proceedings of the 25th Annual meeting of the Association for Natural Language Processing*, pages 550–553. (in Japanese).

Sebastien Jean, Stanislas Lauly, Orhan Firat, and Kyunghyun Cho. 2017. Does neural machine translation benefit from larger context? *arXiv preprint arXiv:1704.05135*.

Melvin Johnson, Mike Schuster, Quoc V. Le, Maxim Krikun, Yonghui Wu, Zhifeng Chen, Nikhil Thorat, Fernanda Viégas, Martin Wattenberg, Greg Corrado, Macduff Hughes, and Jeffrey Dean. 2017. Google's multilingual neural machine translation system: Enabling zero-shot translation. *Transactions of the Association for Computational Linguistics (TACL)*, 5:339–351.

Diederik P Kingma and Jimmy Ba. 2015. Adam: A method for stochastic optimization. In *Proceedings of the the third International Conference for Learning Representations (ICLR)*.

Philipp Koehn. 2005. Europarl: A parallel corpus for statistical machine translation. In *The tenth Machine Translation Summit (MT Summit X)*, pages 79–86.

Pierre Lison and Jörg Tiedemann. 2016. OpenSubtitles2016: Extracting large parallel corpora from movie and TV subtitles. In *Proceedings of the tenth International Conference on Language Resources and Evaluation (LREC)*, pages 923–929.

Sameen Maruf and Gholamreza Haffari. 2018. Document context neural machine translation with memory networks. In *Proceedings of the 56th Annual Meeting of the Association for Computational Linguistics (ACL)*, pages 1275–1284.

Sameen Maruf, André F. T. Martins, and Gholamreza Haffari. 2019. Selective attention for context-aware neural machine translation. In *Proceedings of the 2019 Conference of the North American Chapter of the Association for Computational Linguistics: Human Language Technologies (NAACL-HLT))*, pages 3092–3102.

Lesly Miculicich, Dhananjay Ram, Nikolaos Pappas, and James Henderson. 2018. Document-level neural machine translation with hierarchical attention networks. In *Proceedings of the 2018 Conference on Empirical Methods in Natural Language Processing (EMNLP)*, pages 2947–2954.

Mathias Müller, Annette Rios, Elena Voita, and Rico Sennrich. 2018. A large-scale test set for the evaluation of context-aware pronoun translation in neural machine translation. In *Proceedings of the Third Conference on Machine Translation (WMT)*, pages 61–72.

Masaaki Nagata and Makoto Morishita. 2019. An evaluation metric for Japanese to English context-aware machine translation. In *Proceedings of the 25th Annual meeting of the Association for Natural Language Processing*, pages 1–4. (in Japanese).

Toshiaki Nakazawa, Manabu Yaguchi, Kiyotaka Uchimoto, Masao Utiyama, Eiichiro Sumita, Sadao Kurohashi, and Hitoshi Isahara. 2016. ASPEC: Asian scientific paper excerpt corpus. In *Proceedings of the tenth International Conference on Language Resources and Evaluation (LREC)*, pages 2204–2208.

Kishore Papineni, Salim Roukos, Todd Ward, and Wei-Jing Zhu. 2002. BLEU: a method for automatic evaluation of machine translation. In *Proceedings of the 40th annual meeting on association for computational linguistics (ACL)*, pages 311–318.

Reid Pryzant, Youngjoo Chung, Dan Jurafsky, and Denny Britz. 2018. JESC: Japanese-English subtitle corpus. In *Proceedings of the Eleventh International Conference on Language Resources and Evaluation (LREC)*, pages 1133–1137.

Rico Sennrich, Barry Haddow, and Alexandra Birch. 2016a. Improving neural machine translation models with monolingual data. In *Proceedings of the 54th Annual Meeting of the Association for Computational Linguistics (ACL)*, pages 86–96.

Rico Sennrich, Barry Haddow, and Alexandra Birch. 2016b. Neural machine translation of rare words with subword units. In *Proceedings of the 54th Annual Meeting of the Association for Computational Linguistics (ACL)*, pages 1715–1725.

Jörg Tiedemann and Yves Scherrer. 2017. Neural machine translation with extended context. In *Proceedings of the Third Workshop on Discourse in Machine Translation (DiscoMT)*, pages 82–92.

Zhaopeng Tu, Yang Liu, Shuming Shi, and Tong Zhang. 2018. Learning to remember translation history with a continuous cache. *Transactions of the Association of Computational Linguistics (TACL)*, 6:407–420.

Ashish Vaswani, Noam Shazeer, Niki Parmar, Jakob Uszkoreit, Llion Jones, Aidan N Gomez, Łukasz Kaiser, and Illia Polosukhin. 2017. Attention is all you need. In *Advances in Neural Information Processing Systems 30 (NIPS 2017)*, pages 5998–6008.

Elena Voita, Rico Sennrich, and Ivan Titov. 2019. When a good translation is wrong in context: context-aware machine translation improves on deixis, ellipsis, and lexical cohesion. In *Proceedings of the 57th Annual Meeting of the Association for Computational Linguistics (ACL)*, pages 1198–1212.

Elena Voita, Pavel Serdyukov, Rico Sennrich, and Ivan Titov. 2018. Context-aware neural machine translation learns anaphora resolution. In *Proceedings of the 56th Annual Meeting of the Association for Computational Linguistics (ACL)*, pages 1264–1274.

Longyue Wang, Zhaopeng Tu, Andy Way, and Qun Liu. 2017. Exploiting cross-sentence context for neural machine translation. In *Proceedings of the 2017 Conference on Empirical Methods in Natural Language Processing (EMNLP)*, pages 2826–2831.

Yukun Zhu, Ryan Kiros, Rich Zemel, Ruslan Salakhutdinov, Raquel Urtasun, Antonio Torralba, and Sanja Fidler. 2015. Aligning books and movies: Towards story-like visual explanations by watching movies and reading books. In *Proceedings of the IEEE International Conference on Computer Vision (ICCV)*, pages 19–27.

Context-aware Neural Machine Translation with Coreference Information

Takumi Ohtani[†], **Hidetaka Kamigaito**[†],
Masaaki Nagata[‡] and **Manabu Okumura**[†]
[†] Institute of Innovative Research, Tokyo Institute of Technology
[‡] NTT Communication Science Laboratories, NTT Corporation
{ohtani, kamigaito}@lr.pi.titech.ac.jp, masaaki.nagata.et@hco.ntt.co.jp, oku@pi.titech.ac.jp

Abstract

We present neural machine translation models for translating a sentence in a text by using a graph-based encoder which can consider coreference relations provided within the text explicitly. The graph-based encoder can dynamically encode the source text without attending to all tokens in the text. In experiments, our proposed models provide statistically significant improvement to the previous approach of at most 0.9 points in the BLEU score on the OpenSubtitle2018 English-to-Japanese data set. Experimental results also show that the graph-based encoder can handle a longer text well, compared with the previous approach.

1 Introduction

The quality of machine translators has recently dramatically improved with Sequence-to-Sequence (Seq2Seq) models (Bahdanau et al., 2014). Most Seq2Seq models are used based on the premise that each sentence is independently translated one by one. In contrast to this premise, real sentences are often an element of a larger unit, such as a document. This means that a sentence is not always semantically self-contained in itself. To correctly interpret a sentence which is a part of a document, it is important to consider its context, preceding and/or succeeding sentences.

In order to tackle the problem, Seq2Seq models that can receive two sentences (Tiedemann and Scherrer, 2017; Bawden et al., 2018; Voita et al., 2018; Wang et al., 2017) have been utilized. For capturing multiple-sentence information more effectively, Miculicich et al. (2018); Zhang et al. (2018) incorporated document-level attention modules into Seq2Seq models. Stojanovski and Fraser (2018) proposed a Seq2Seq model which can capture antecedents of pronouns in the previous source sentence by using a coreference resolution toolkit. To capture the entire source text information, these models strongly depend on attention distributions.

However, the space complexity of the attention mechanism in the Seq2Seq model increases in proportion to the square of the input sequence length, because it tries to attend to all the words in the source text. This characteristic prevents the model from translating a long text. Furthermore, in translating into a pro-drop language such as Japanese, longer contexts are required to generate accurate and naturally concise sentences.

To avoid the problem, we propose a model that can effectively capture contextual information, preceding and succeeding sentences of the source sentence to be translated, by constructing an encoder that is based on explicit coreference relations. The proposed model can directly take into account relationships between sentences via a graph structured encoder constructed with a coreference resolution toolkit. Therefore, it does not need to attend to all input tokens. This characteristic enables our proposed model to handle more sentences in a step, compared with the previous models, and it may improve translation quality when a source text has many sentences.

Experimental results on English-to-Japanese translation pairs in OpenSubtitles2018 (Lison et al., 2018) show that our proposed model can significantly improve the previous model in terms of BLEU scores. In addition, we observe that our model is especially effective in translating a sentence which is a part of a long text, compared to the previous model.

2 Sequence-to-Sequence Model

In this section, we explain the standard Seq2Seq model proposed by Bahdanau et al. (2014), which

Proceedings of the Fourth Workshop on Discourse in Machine Translation (DiscoMT 2019), pages 45–50
Hong Kong, China, November 3, 2019.

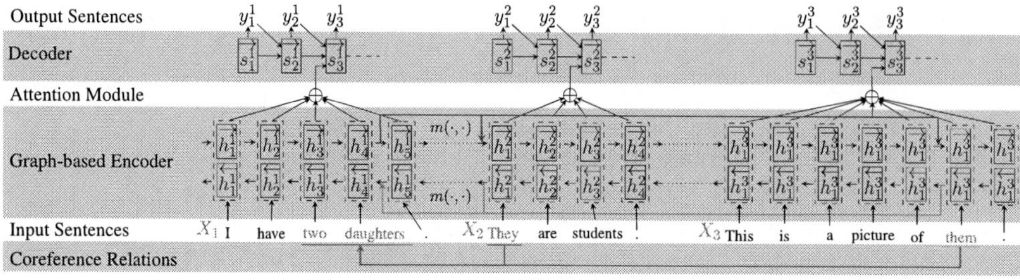

Figure 1: Network structure of the proposed model. Blue arrows indicate a forward hidden state merge operation and green arrows indicate a backward hidden state merge operation. Both operations are based on a coreference relation represented as red arrows. Attention distributions are calculated only on a currently translating sentence.

our proposed model is based on. We use LSTM (Hochreiter and Schmidhuber, 1997) as recurrent neural network (RNN) structures in the encoder and the decoder. In the Seq2Seq model, a probability of translating an input sentence $\mathbf{x} = (x_1, \cdots, x_{T_x})$ into an output sentence $\mathbf{y} = (y_1, \cdots, y_n)$ is represented as follows:

$$
\begin{aligned}
p\left(y_i | y_1, \ldots, y_{i-1}, \mathbf{x}\right) &= softmax(g\left(s_i, d_i\right)), \\
s_i &= dec\left(s_{i-1}, emb(y_{i-1}), d_i\right), \\
d_i &= \sum_{j=1}^{T_x} a\left(s_{i-1}, h_j\right) h_j, \\
h_t &= enc\left(emb(x_t), h_{t-1}, h_{t+1}\right),
\end{aligned} \tag{1}
$$

where i is the position of an output token, t is the position of an input token, $emb(\cdot)$ is a function that returns the embedding of an input word, g is a 2-layer feedforward neural network (FFNN), dec is a decoder forward-LSTM, enc is an encoder bidirectional-LSTM (Bi-LSTM), and a is a dot attention (Luong et al., 2015) for calculating the attention weight.

3 Graph-based Encoder with Coreference Relations

Our proposed model can encode not only the sentence to be translated but also its preceding and succeeding sentences together, based on the results of coreference resolution. Therefore, information about sentence relationships can be effectively utilized. Figure1 shows the network structure of our proposed model. At first, input sentences are analyzed by using a coreference resolution system. After that, the encoder part is structured based on the coreference resolution results, and the input text is encoded into hidden states. Then, the hidden states are converted to a translated text via attention distributions and the decoder. During the translation, the attention distributions are only calculated for the currently translated sentence. In the next subsections, we explain the details of each step. We denote a sequence of N sentences as $(X_1, \cdots, X_N)$, and j-th word in X_i as x^i_j hereafter.

3.1 Coreference Resolution

Multiple sentences in a source text $(X_1, \cdots, X_N)$ are concatenated and then input to a coreference resolution system. We use NeuralCoref[1] as the coreference resolution system. Let the length of X_i be T_i. The concatenated token sequence is represented as:

$$
(x^1_1, \cdots, x^1_{T_1}, x^2_1, \cdots, x^2_{T_2}, \cdots, x^N_1, \cdots, x^N_{T_N}). \tag{2}
$$

The coreference resolution system extracts N_c clusters of coreferring mentions $(c_1, \cdots, c_{N_c})$, which are defined as:

$$
c_k = (main_k, sub_k), \tag{3}
$$

where $main_k$ is a span of the representative mention in a cluster of coreferring mentions, and sub_k is a span of another mention in the cluster.[2] In general, because many mentions are in a single cluster, the same $main_k$ is sometimes paired to different mentions.

To use coreference relations in our graph-based encoder, we need to consider word-based coreference relations. Let $head(\cdot)$ be a function that returns the first word of an input span and $tail(\cdot)$ be a function that returns the last word of the input span. When x^i_j refers to $x^{i'}_{j'}$, x^i_j and $x^{i'}_{j'}$ satisfy the following conditions:

$$
\begin{aligned}
x^{i'}_{j'} &= tail(main_k), \\
x^i_j &= head(sub_k).
\end{aligned} \tag{4}
$$

[1] https://github.com/huggingface/neuralcoref. This code is based on the work by Clark and Manning (2016).

[2] We treat a nominal noun which is the antecedent of a pronoun or a proper noun as a representative mention.

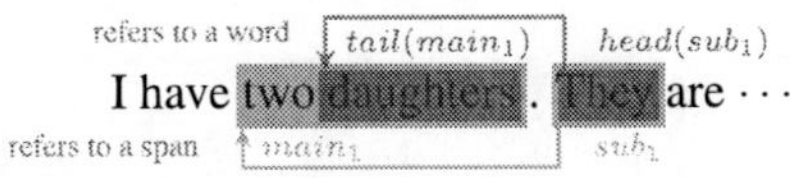

Figure 2: An example of a word-based coreference relation.

Figure 2 shows an example of a word-based coreference relation.

Furthermore, we denote a set of words which are referred by word x^i_j as $ref(x^i_j)$. Because the number of words referred by a word is at most one, the number of elements in $ref(x^i_j)$ is either 1 or 0. $ref(x^i_j)$ can be divided into either anaphora, $ref_f(x^i_j)$, or cataphora, $ref_b(x^i_j)$, as follows:

$$\begin{aligned} ref_f(x^i_j) &= \{(i',j') \in ref(x^i_j) | i' < i \lor (i' = i \land j' < j)\}, \\ ref_b(x^i_j) &= \{(i',j') \in ref(x^i_j) | i' > i \lor (i' = i \land j' > j)\}, \end{aligned} \quad (5)$$

where $(i',j') \in ref(x^i_j)$ represents a reference from x^i_j to $x^{i'}_{j'}$. The ref_f and ref_b are used to decide the network structure of the encoder part in the proposed model.

3.2 Graph-based Encoder

In this section, we explain how to use the coreference relations in the encoder. Similar to the standard Seq2Seq model, the encoder of the proposed model is based on Bi-LSTM. For each input sentence $X_i = (x^i_1, \cdots)$, the forward encoder calculates the current hidden state $\overrightarrow{h}^i_t$ at the position of a word x^i_t as follows:

$$\overrightarrow{h}^i_t = \overrightarrow{LSTM}\left(emb(x^i_t), m(\overrightarrow{h}^i_{t-1}, ref_f(x^i_t))\right), \quad (6)$$

where $\overrightarrow{h}^i_{t-1}$ is the previous hidden state, $ref_f(x^i_t)$ is a set of words which are referred by x^i_t and $m(\cdot,\cdot)$ is a function which merges hidden state vectors. In this paper, we propose the following two functions as $m(\cdot,\cdot)$:

Coref-mean treats averaged hidden state vectors as the merged vector, as follows:

$$m(\overrightarrow{h}^i_{t-1}, ref_f(x^i_t)) = \frac{1}{|ref_f(x^i_t)|+1}(\overrightarrow{h}^i_{t-1} + \sum_{(i',j') \in ref_f(x^i_t)} \overrightarrow{h}^{i'}_{j'}). \quad (7)$$

Coref-gate treats weighted sum of the hidden state vectors as the merged vector, as follows:

$$m(\overrightarrow{h}^i_{t-1}, ref_f(x^i_t)) = \overrightarrow{h}^i_{t-1} + \sum_{(i',j') \in ref_f(x^i_t)} \beta^{i'}_{j'} \odot \overrightarrow{h}^{i'}_{j'}, \quad (8)$$

where $\odot$ represents the element product for each dimension and $\beta^{i'}_{j'}$ represents the importance of $\overrightarrow{h}^{i'}_{j'}$. $\beta^{i'}_{j'}$ is calculated as follows:

$$\beta^{i'}_{j'} = sigmoid(W_t \overrightarrow{h}^{i'}_{j'} + W_s \overrightarrow{h}^i_{t-1}), \quad (9)$$

where W_t and W_s are weight matrices.

The backward encoding is similarly processed by replacing ref_f with ref_b. Finally, the forward and backward hidden states are concatenated to $h^i_t = [\overrightarrow{h}^i_t; \overleftarrow{h}^i_t]$ for each t. After that, h^i_t is used for translation, in place of h_t in equation (1), with attending only to the target sentence to be translated.

4 Experiments

4.1 Experimental Setting

We evaluated the proposed models on the English-to-Japanese translation data set in OpenSubtitles2018 (Lison et al., 2018). We cut out consecutive n $(= 1, 2, 3, 5, 7)$ sentences from the original data set as a unit. After that, we randomly selected 2000 units as test data, and the remaining about 1.87 million units were used as training data. All Japanese texts were tokenized by MeCab[3] with NEologd (Sato et al., 2017).

We set the vocabulary size for both source and target sides as 32,000. Both the encoder and the decoder were composed of 2-layer LSTMs. The dimension size of word embeddings for both source and target sides was set to 500. The dimension size of the encoder LSTM layers, the decoder LSTM layers, and an attention layer were set to 500, 1000, and 500, respectively. Initial values for weights were randomly sampled from a uniform distribution within the range of -1 to 1 (Glorot and Bengio, 2010).

Adam (Kingma and Ba, 2014) was used to update weight parameters, and the learning rate was set to 0.001. Learning was carried out for 200,000 steps for the entire training data. The mini-batch size was set to 32, and the gradients were averaged by the number of examples in each mini-batch. The order of mini-batches was randomly shuffled at the start of the training. Pytorch was used to implement the models. All models were run on a single GPU NVIDIA Tesla P100[4] independently.

We changed the number of input sentences, n, in the range of $\{1, 2, 3, 5, 7\}$ to observe the relationships between translation quality and the number of input sentences. We input a sentence to be

[3]http://taku910.github.io/mecab/

[4]This device has a 16GB memory.

	Number of sentences (n)				
	1	*2*	*3*	*5*	*7*
Cor-m	7.84	8.06	8.33	8.65	8.68
Cor-g	7.96	8.46	8.60	8.75	**8.79**
Cor-g-c	-	-	8.58	8.73	8.70
Concat	7.69	7.90	7.91	7.81	×

Table 1: BLEU scores for each model. The bold indicates the best score. The underlined indicates that these scores are statistically significantly improved from the score of the baseline Concat at the same setting ($p < 0.05$). × represents that the model did not run due to the shortage of GPU memories.

$n = 1$	$n = 2$	$n = 3$	$n = 5$	$n = 7$
12.8%	13.2%	13.8%	14.6%	15.4%

Table 2: The percentage of sentences containing coreferences in the test set.

translated and $n - 1$ sentences that precede the input sentence.

As a baseline model, we used a method concatenating multiple input sentences and generating a single sentence, proposed by Bawden et al. (2018) (**Concat**)[5]. We compared our proposed models, Coref-mean (**Cor-m**) and Coref-gate (**Cor-g**), with the baseline. In order to evaluate the effectiveness of succeeding sentences, we also experimented with the cases of inputting the same number of preceding and succeeding sentences for the target sentence to be translated at the center, for **Cor-g**. We denote this setting as Coref-gate-centered (**Cor-g-c**). The number of weight parameters for each model is 111,057k for the baseline and **Cor-m**, and 111,558k for **Cor-g**.

We used BLEU scores (Papineni et al., 2002) to evaluate the translation performance for each model. All reported BLEU scores in the experiments are averages for three times and are based on MeCab tokenization. Significance tests were conducted by paired bootstrap resampling (Koehn, 2004) with multevel (Clark et al., 2011)[6].

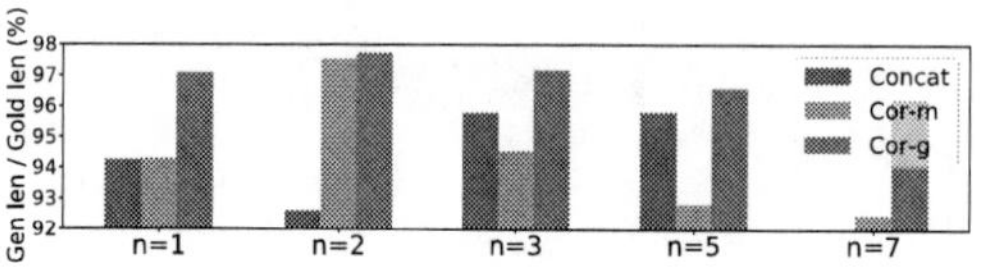

Figure 3: The ratio of token numbers in generated translations to those in reference translations.

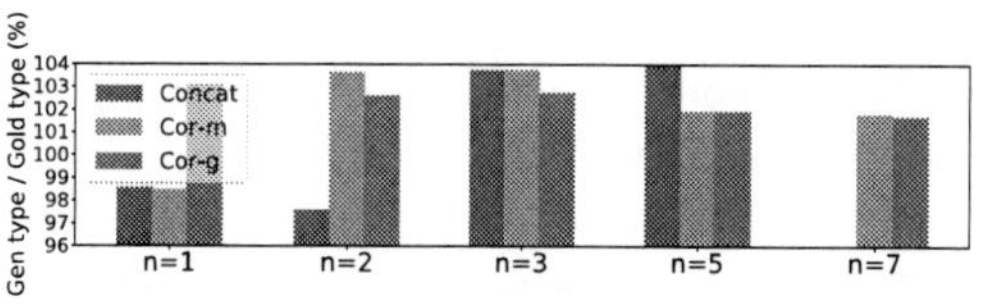

Figure 4: The ratio of token types in generated translations to those in reference translations.

4.2 Results and Analysis

Table 1 shows the results[7]. In this table, we can observe that our proposed models, **Cor-m** and **Cor-g**, outperformed the baseline **Concat** in terms of BLEU scores at every unit length. Interestingly, at the setting of $n = 1$, **Cor-g** also outperformed **Concat**. As shown in Table 2, this is because our proposed models can also use inter-sentential coreference information for translation. In the setting of $n = 2$, all the results improved from those for $n = 1$. This is consistent to the reported results in Bawden et al. (2018). In the setting of $n > 2$, improvement of BLEU scores for **Concat** stopped at $n = 3$, in contrast to the proposed models. This indicates that the proposed model can handle more sentences well by using their graph-based encoder and provided coreference information.

The scores for **Cor-g** is always better than those for **Cor-m**. From this result, we can say that the gating mechanism in **Cor-g** works well. In addition, as shown in Figure 3, the translation of **Cor-g** has a closer token length to the reference, while **Concat** and **Cor-m** encounter severe undergeneration problems. The results in Figure 4 show that in $n > 2$, **Cor-g** can maintain word coherence without increasing word types in generated sentences. Taking into account the gain of the BLEU scores, these results support our estimation that **Cor-g** can capture contexts well, compared to **Cor-m** and **Concat**.

However, the scores for **Cor-g-c** degraded compared to **Cor-g** at the same sentence numbers. This result reflects a tendency that most coreferences

[5]In our preliminary comparison, there are no statistically significant differences in translation performances between **Concat** and the method of inputting and outputting concatenated multiple sentences, also proposed by Bawden et al. (2018). From the computational efficiency perspective, therefore, we chose **Concat** as our baseline.

[6]https://github.com/jhclark/multeval

[7]These results are close to the reported BLEU scores of the Ja-En caption translations in Pryzant et al. (2018)

are anaphora, and cataphora is rarely observed in the test set. Ignoring the succeeding sentences, **Cor-g-c** at $n = 3, 5, 7$ is similar to the setting of **Cor-g** with $n = 2, 3, 4$. Interestingly, **Cor-g-c** at $n = 3, 5$ achieved better BLEU scores, compared to **Cor-g** with $n = 2, 3$. This indicates that cataphora information is also useful to translate many sentences in a text.

5 Conclusion

In this paper, we proposed a Seq2Seq model that can incorporate information in preceding and succeeding sentences of the translating sentence effectively, by taking into account provided coreference relations explicitly. Experimental results showed that the proposed models can improve the translation quality in the setting of inputting multiple sentences jointly, compared to the previous model. From these results, we could conclude that considering explicit coreference relations in the Seq2Seq model actually contributes to improve the performances on the English-to-Japanese translation.

References

Dzmitry Bahdanau, Kyunghyun Cho, and Yoshua Bengio. 2014. Neural machine translation by jointly learning to align and translate. *arXiv e-prints*, abs/1409.0473.

Rachel Bawden, Rico Sennrich, Alexandra Birch, and Barry Haddow. 2018. Evaluating discourse phenomena in neural machine translation. In *Proceedings of the 2018 Conference of the North American Chapter of the Association for Computational Linguistics: Human Language Technologies, Volume 1 (Long Papers)*, pages 1304–1313. Association for Computational Linguistics.

Jonathan H. Clark, Chris Dyer, Alon Lavie, and Noah A. Smith. 2011. Better hypothesis testing for statistical machine translation: Controlling for optimizer instability. In *Proceedings of the 49th Annual Meeting of the Association for Computational Linguistics: Human Language Technologies*, pages 176–181, Portland, Oregon, USA. Association for Computational Linguistics.

Kevin Clark and Christopher D. Manning. 2016. Deep reinforcement learning for mention-ranking coreference models. In *Proceedings of the 2016 Conference on Empirical Methods in Natural Language Processing*, pages 2256–2262, Austin, Texas. Association for Computational Linguistics.

Xavier Glorot and Yoshua Bengio. 2010. Understanding the difficulty of training deep feedforward neural networks. In *Proceedings of the International Conference on Artificial Intelligence and Statistics (AISTATS10). Society for Artificial Intelligence and Statistics*.

Sepp Hochreiter and Jürgen Schmidhuber. 1997. Long short-term memory. *Neural Comput.*, 9(8):1735–1780.

Diederik P. Kingma and Jimmy Ba. 2014. Adam: A method for stochastic optimization. *CoRR*, abs/1412.6980.

Philipp Koehn. 2004. Statistical significance tests for machine translation evaluation. In *Proceedings of EMNLP 2004*, pages 388–395, Barcelona, Spain. Association for Computational Linguistics.

Pierre Lison, Jörg Tiedemann, and Milen Kouylekov. 2018. Opensubtitles2018: Statistical rescoring of sentence alignments in large, noisy parallel corpora. In *Proceedings of the Eleventh International Conference on Language Resources and Evaluation (LREC-2018)*. European Language Resource Association.

Thang Luong, Hieu Pham, and Christopher D. Manning. 2015. Effective approaches to attention-based neural machine translation. In *Proceedings of the 2015 Conference on Empirical Methods in Natural Language Processing*, pages 1412–1421. Association for Computational Linguistics.

Lesly Miculicich, Dhananjay Ram, Nikolaos Pappas, and James Henderson. 2018. Document-level neural machine translation with hierarchical attention networks. In *Proceedings of the 2018 Conference on Empirical Methods in Natural Language Processing*, pages 2947–2954, Brussels, Belgium. Association for Computational Linguistics.

Kishore Papineni, Salim Roukos, Todd Ward, and Wei-Jing Zhu. 2002. Bleu: a method for automatic evaluation of machine translation. In *Proceedings of 40th Annual Meeting of the Association for Computational Linguistics*, pages 311–318, Philadelphia, Pennsylvania, USA. Association for Computational Linguistics.

Reid Pryzant, Youngjoo Chung, Dan Jurafsky, and Denny Britz. 2018. JESC: Japanese-English subtitle corpus. In *Proceedings of the Eleventh International Conference on Language Resources and Evaluation (LREC-2018)*, Miyazaki, Japan. European Languages Resources Association (ELRA).

Toshinori Sato, Taiichi Hashimoto, and Manabu Okumura. 2017. Implementation of a word segmentation dictionary called mecab-ipadic-neologd and study on how to use it effectively for information retrieval (in japanese). In *NLP*, pages NLP2017-B6-1. The Association for Natural Language Processing.

Dario Stojanovski and Alexander Fraser. 2018. Coreference and coherence in neural machine translation: A study using oracle experiments. In *Proceedings of the Third Conference on Machine Translation: Research Papers*, pages 49–60, Belgium, Brussels. Association for Computational Linguistics.

Jörg Tiedemann and Yves Scherrer. 2017. Neural machine translation with extended context. In *Proceedings of the Third Workshop on Discourse in Machine Translation*, pages 82–92, Copenhagen, Denmark. Association for Computational Linguistics.

Elena Voita, Pavel Serdyukov, Rico Sennrich, and Ivan Titov. 2018. Context-aware neural machine translation learns anaphora resolution. In *Proceedings of the 56th Annual Meeting of the Association for Computational Linguistics (Volume 1: Long Papers)*, pages 1264–1274. Association for Computational Linguistics.

Longyue Wang, Zhaopeng Tu, Andy Way, and Qun Liu. 2017. Exploiting cross-sentence context for neural machine translation. In *Proceedings of the 2017 Conference on Empirical Methods in Natural Language Processing*, pages 2826–2831, Copenhagen, Denmark. Association for Computational Linguistics.

Jiacheng Zhang, Huanbo Luan, Maosong Sun, Feifei Zhai, Jingfang Xu, Min Zhang, and Yang Liu. 2018. Improving the transformer translation model with document-level context. In *Proceedings of the 2018 Conference on Empirical Methods in Natural Language Processing*, pages 533–542, Brussels, Belgium. Association for Computational Linguistics.

Analysing concatenation approaches to document-level NMT in two different domains

Yves Scherrer[1] **Jörg Tiedemann**[1] **Sharid Loáiciga**[2]
[1]Department of Digital Humanities, University of Helsinki
[2]CLASP, Dept. of Philosophy, Linguistics and Theory of Science, University of Gothenburg
yves.scherrer@helsinki.fi jorg.tiedemann@helsinki.fi
sharid.loaiciga@gu.se

Abstract

In this paper, we investigate how different aspects of discourse context affect the performance of recent neural MT systems. We describe two popular datasets covering news and movie subtitles and we provide a thorough analysis of the distribution of various document-level features in their domains. Furthermore, we train a set of context-aware MT models on both datasets and propose a comparative evaluation scheme that contrasts coherent context with artificially scrambled documents and absent context, arguing that the impact of discourse-aware MT models will become visible in this way. Our results show that the models are indeed affected by the manipulation of the test data, providing a different view on document-level translation quality than absolute sentence-level scores.

1 Introduction

Shortly after the change of paradigm in Machine Translation (MT) from statistical to neural architectures, the interest in discourse phenomena flourished again. This is not by chance, as neural models can embed larger text spans into contextual representations and can be set up to learn relevant features from the raw data to produce better translations.

It is still unclear though how the impact of discourse on MT quality should be evaluated and analyzed. On one side, it is difficult to pinpoint particular contextual features that neural MT (NMT) models are picking up. On the other, it is difficult to judge good translations purely in terms of discourse features. In this paper, we investigate the discourse-related biases in data. Our contributions are twofold:

- we provide a thorough analysis of two popular machine translation datasets in terms of document-level features,
- we train different context-aware MT models (Tiedemann and Scherrer, 2017; Agrawal et al., 2018; Maruf et al., 2019; Junczys-Dowmunt, 2019) on the two datasets and evaluate them using a comparative setup with artificially scrambled data.

As discourse properties of the data, we consider pronouns and coreference chains, connectives, and negation. For the evaluation of translation quality and the influence of document-level context, we contrast context-aware models at test time with (1) clean coherent text, (2) incoherent input and (3) zero-context input.[1] For the second type, we scramble sentences and insert document boundaries at arbitrary positions in the test data. For the third approach, we add document boundaries after each test instance. This setup provides a cheap way of testing the influence of contextual information on translation performance that can be measured in common ways, for example, facilitating automatic evaluation metrics such as BLEU or METEOR.

2 Related work

2.1 Discourse

Research about discourse and MT has shifted from explicitly enhancing systems with discourse knowledge to evaluating how much the systems have learned specific discourse features through different resources, test suites being a popular one (cf. Sim Smith, 2017; Popescu-Belis, 2019). Throughout, however, particular discourse phenomena are consistently targeted, as they are indeed indicators of globally good, cohesive and coherent texts. Pronouns (Hardmeier and Federico, 2010; Guillou, 2012; Hardmeier et al., 2013;

[1]*Context* here refers to text outside of the sentence to be translated.

Proceedings of the Fourth Workshop on Discourse in Machine Translation (DiscoMT 2019), pages 51–61
Hong Kong, China, November 3, 2019.

Guillou and Hardmeier, 2016; Müller et al., 2018; Guillou et al., 2018) have been largely at the center of attention, and more recently the translation of pronouns in the context of their coreferential chains has been looked at (Lapshinova-Koltunski and Hardmeier, 2017; Voita et al., 2018; Lapshinova-Koltunski et al., 2019). Other devices studied are verbal tenses (Gong et al., 2012; Loáiciga et al., 2014; Ramm and Fraser, 2016) and connectives (Meyer et al., 2012; Meyer and Popescu-Belis, 2012), although not using neural models. Motivated by approximating the ability of systems to grasp more abstract properties related to coherence, ambiguous words have also been targeted (Rios Gonzales et al., 2017; Bawden et al., 2018; Rios et al., 2018), as well as ellipsis (Voita et al., 2019). Last, negation (Fancellu and Webber, 2015) is a rather understudied phenomenon, but like pronouns and their antecedents, the scope of the negation can be in a different sentence.

In this paper we investigate these features in the training data and assess translation using standard automatic metrics and a data scrambling strategy.

2.2 Context-aware NMT

Tiedemann and Scherrer (2017) present a simple approach to context-aware NMT: instead of training the model on pairs of single source and target sentences, they add sentences from the left context to the sentence to be translated, either only on the source side or both on source and target sides. These models are evaluated on a German–English corpus extracted from OpenSubtitles, and the best results are obtained with two source sentences and one target sentence. Agrawal et al. (2018) extend these experiments by considering additional contexts. They evaluate their work on the IWSLT 2017 dataset for English–Italian, which consists of transcripts of TED talks.

In 2019, the WMT conference featured for the first time a document-level translation task for English–German (Barrault et al., 2019). One of the best-performing systems (Junczys-Dowmunt, 2019) is based on a similar idea: all sentences of a document are concatenated and translated as a whole. Documents whose length exceeds the maximum sequence length defined by the model are simply split.

The approaches outlined above, which we refer to as "concatenation models", do not require any change to the NMT model architecture. Other recent work explores the feasability of extending NMT models to make them context-aware. A common approach is to use additional encoders for the context sentence(s) with a modified attention mechanism (Jean et al., 2017; Bawden et al., 2018; Voita et al., 2018). Another technique (Miculicich et al., 2018; Maruf et al., 2019) explores the integration of context through a hierarchical architecture which models the contextual information in a structured manner using word-level and sentence-level abstractions.

The different models have been evaluated on different language pairs and different datasets. In this paper, we focus on a single language pair, English–German (in both directions), and on two textual domains: news translation and movie subtitles translation. For the news translation task (denoted as *WMT*) we rely on the established setup of WMT 2019[2] with the Newstest2018 data as our dedicated test set. For the movie subtitles (referred to as *OST*), we use data from the OpenSubtitles corpus released on OPUS[3] with our own split into training, development and test data. More details about the data and our setup will be given in the following section.

3 Two datasets for English–German document-level translation

Different text genres and types exhibit different types of discourse-level properties. The choice of training corpus therefore determines what features a NMT model can potentially learn, and the choice of test corpus determines which features can be reliably evaluated. Our experiments are based on two datasets that cover the same language pair, but very different textual characteristics.

The **OST** dataset is built from the English–German part of the publicly available OpenSubtitles2016 corpus (Lison and Tiedemann, 2016). Of the 16,910 movies and TV series in the collection, 16,510 are used for training, and 4 each are held out for development and testing purposes. Each movie is considered a single document. It corresponds to the dataset used in Tiedemann and Scherrer (2017). General properties of this dataset can be found in Table 1.

The **WMT** dataset comprises the subset of corpora allowed at the WMT 2019 news translation

[2] See `http://www.statmt.org/wmt19/translation-task.html`.

[3] `http://opus.nlpl.eu/OpenSubtitles2016.php`

Corpus	Documents	Sentences	Sents/Doc	Tokens DE	Tokens EN	Tokens/Sent
OST Train	16,510	13,544k	820	104,447k	111,729k	8.0
OST Valid	4	5k	1249	41k	43k	8.4
OST Test	4	5k	1249	38k	47k	8.4
WMT Train	583,358	12,690k	22	259,384k	276,401k	21.1
WMT Valid	236	5k	22	106k	111k	21.1
WMT Test	122	3k	25	64k	68k	21.9

Table 1: General characteristics of the two datasets. Tokens/Sent values are averaged over the DE and EN tokens.

task which contains document boundaries. The training set includes parallel data from the Europarl v9, NewsCommentary v14, and Rapid2019 collections. We select the Newstest2015 and Newstest2016 corpora as our validation set and the Newstest2018 corpus as our test set. General properties of this dataset can be found in Table 1.

Table 1 shows that the two datasets are comparable in terms of sentence numbers.[4] However, the documents in OST are up to 50 times larger than those in WMT (cf. column *Sents/Doc*). On the other hand, WMT sentences are more than twice as long than OST sentences (cf. column *Tokens/Sent*), which is in line with our expectations.

A third dataset based on transcripts of TED talks (Cettolo et al., 2012), has also been used for document-level translation (Agrawal et al., 2018). We do not consider this dataset for training due to its smaller size, but use the PROTEST test suite, which is based on this corpus, for evaluation (Guillou and Hardmeier, 2016; Guillou et al., 2018).

3.1 Discourse-level properties

In recent literature, various linguistic features have been identified to contribute to document-level coherence and cohesion. In this section, we assess the two datasets in order to estimate their suitability and difficulty for document-level translation. We investigate the following phenomena:

Pronouns: We first extract a list of pronouns per language by tagging the training corpora with SpaCy[5], extracting the tokens labeled as PRON and manually cleaning the resulting list (cf. Table 7). Then, the frequency of pronouns is computed independently for English and German.

The results in Table 2 show that about every 10th word of the OST corpus is a pronoun, whereas pronouns are three to four times rarer in the WMT corpus.[6] This divergence is to be expected, as OST consists mainly of dialogues.

Not all pronouns are intrinsically hard to translate. Therefore, we also examine how many **ambiguous pronouns** occur in the corpora. To this end, the English and German corpora are word-aligned using Eflomal (Östling and Tiedemann, 2016) and for each source pronoun (as defined in the list extracted previously), the target pronouns are retrieved. If this list contains at least two words totalling each at least 10% of occurrences, we consider the source pronoun as ambiguous (cf. Table 7). This feature is computed separately for both translation directions.

On average, about half of the pronoun occurrences are ambiguous, with most ambiguities concerning case (e.g. *me* translating both to accusative *mich* and dative *mir*). The English pronouns in the OST dataset deviate from this tendency, mainly because of the prevalence of *you*: this pronoun is ambiguous both in terms of number and politeness and can be translated as *du*, *ihr*, or *Sie* (see also Sennrich et al., 2016).

Connectives: As part of their *Accuracy of Connective Translation* metric, Hajlaoui and Popescu-Belis (2013) provide a list of eight ambiguous English connectives and their German translations. We count the number of sentence pairs that contain both an English connective and one of its German translations, regardless of its associated sense.

Ambiguous connectives show an inverse frequency distribution compared to pronouns: they are about ten times as frequent in WMT than in OST. This divergence can again be attributed to genre differences.

[4]By sentences, we mean the lines obtained by the sentence alignment process.

[5]spacy.io

[6]The numbers for German are higher because the pronoun list contains more relative and demonstrative pronouns than the English one, as a result of annotation differences in the SpaCy training corpora.

Corpus	Pronouns		Ambiguous pronouns		Ambiguous connectives	Negations		Negation discrep.	Coreference chains		Cross-sent. pron. coref.	
	DE	EN	DE	EN	DE–EN	DE	EN	DE–EN	DE	EN	DE	EN
OST Train	106.0	97.0	44.1	71.1	5.0	151.6	162.8	57.1	290.5	148.3	67.2	44.5
OST Valid	104.7	92.7	49.9	73.0	6.2	165.5	171.5	65.6	346.1	167.5	70.2	46.4
OST Test	101.1	99.3	53.0	69.7	5.8	148.9	191.9	75.0	292.5	178.8	66.8	46.9
WMT Train	36.1	20.0	20.1	13.5	60.2	176.1	176.2	19.6	670.3	495.3	91.9	80.6
WMT Valid	44.2	29.6	24.6	20.8	62.5	182.1	177.2	23.8	693.5	544.2	111.5	97.6
WMT Test	44.0	25.8	25.9	20.0	58.3	167.4	169.1	18.3	726.8	535.0	115.4	99.7
	per thousand tokens				per thousand lines							

Table 2: Discourse-level features in the OST and WMT datasets. Coreference values were computed on a subset of the training corpora.

Negations: We establish a list of sentential and nominal negation words for both languages (cf. Table 7) and count the number of sentences that contain at least one negation word. We also count **negation discrepancies**, i.e. aligned sentence pairs where a negation was identified in one language but not in the other.

While the overall frequencies of negations are similar in both corpora, there are significantly more discrepancies in the OST dataset. These can be ascribed to two factors: free translation (a negation can be paraphrased with expressions such as *fail to*, *doubt if*, etc.), and sentence alignment errors.

Coreference chains: We assume that a large amount of pronouns, connectives and negations do not require access to large contexts for their correct translation, either because they are unambiguous or because the current sentence is sufficient for their disambiguation. To corroborate this assumption, we annotate the English corpora with the Stanford CoreNLP coreference resolver (Manning et al., 2014; Clark and Manning, 2016) and the German corpora with the CorZu coreference resolver (Tuggener, 2016).[7]

We first report the numbers of coreference chains identified by the resolvers. These numbers are hard to compare across languages due to different performance levels of the two resolvers, and translationese factors such as explicitation. However, they confirm the intuition that news text contains more referring entities than movie dialogues.[8]

Second, we count **cross-sentential pronominal coreference chains**, i.e. chains that span at least two sentences, contain at least one third-person pronoun and at least two different mention strings. The results suggest that about every 10th line of the WMT dataset and about every 20th line of the OST dataset contains a pronoun that requires access to the context for its correct translation. Given the overall training data sizes, NMT models should thus be able to pick up this signal.

Overall, the examined discourse-level features show consistent patterns across the training, validation and test sets. This was not necessarily expected for the WMT corpus, whose training set stems from a wide variety of sources.[9]

Three other discourse-level features could have been analyzed as well: We did not include verbal tenses, as we do not expect them to be particularly problematic for the German–English language pair. Likewise, we did not include measures for lexical consistency (Carpuat and Simard, 2012), as this was already reported to be handled well in SMT. Finally, we did not include ellipsis (Voita et al., 2019) as we found it difficult to detect and not very relevant for German.

4 Context-aware MT models

In this paper, our main focus lies on concatenation models as one of the most straightforward and successful approaches to document-level NMT. We train various concatenation models on both datasets and for both translation directions in order to perform a systematic study on this setup.

[7] Due to slow performance, we could only analyze 13% of the English OST, 5% of the English WMT and 5% of the German WMT training sets. We nevertheless believe that the reported proportions are representative of the entire dataset.

[8] Note also that the WMT dataset may benefit from higher recall as the coreference resolution pipelines are typically trained on newswire data.

[9] For the MT training, we shuffle the datasets keeping documents and document boundaries intact.

Inspired by Agrawal et al. (2018), we name the configurations according to the following schema:

$$i\textbf{Prev + Curr + }j\textbf{Next} \rightarrow k\textbf{Prev + Curr}$$

where i denotes the number of previous sentences on the source side, j the number of following sentences on the source side, and k the number of previous sentences on the target side. In all models, only the current sentence is evaluated. The following configurations are tested:

- Curr → Curr (baseline)
- 1Prev + Curr → Curr
- 1Prev + Curr + 1Next → Curr
- 2Prev + Curr → Curr
- 1Prev + Curr → 1Prev + Curr
- 1Prev + Curr + 1Next → 1Prev + Curr

Several discourse-level properties, among which most prominently pronoun gender, also depend on the previously generated output in the target language. Therefore, we also include an oracle variant where we the reference translation of the previous sentence (instead of its source) is fed to the system:

- 1PrevTarget + Curr → Curr

Furthermore, we also train fixed window models as in Junczys-Dowmunt (2019):

- 100T → 100T: A model that sees chunks of at most 100 tokens (after subword encoding) on either source and target side.
- 250T → 250T: A model that sees chunks of at most 250 tokens (after subword encoding) on either source and target side.

Note that these chunks are not produced using a sliding window but rather break documents at arbitrary positions unless they are less than the maximum size in length. We adopt the same annotation scheme as proposed in the original approach, marking segment and document boundaries with special symbols for document-internal breaks and continuations. We never break sentences from the original alignment into pieces, which would negatively affect the model and complicate the alignment of training examples.

The chosen chunk lengths seem very small, especially when considering subword units. Table 3 lists some basic statistics that demonstrate the effect of the chunking approach. We can see that even 100-token windows create reasonably large units that combine context beyond sentence boundaries. For the WMT dataset with larger sentences, we observe an average of almost 3 joined segments per chunk. For the subtitle data, the situation is much more extreme: most segments are very short and a 100-token window corresponds to about 10 segments. Hence, this approach yields a substantial increase of contextual information compared to the baseline.

Window size	Chunks	Sents/chunk
OST training data:		
100 tokens	1 282 985	10.6
250 tokens	496 207	27.3
WMT training data:		
100 tokens	4 286 535	3.0
250 tokens	1 729 601	7.3

Table 3: Basic statistics of fixed-size windows data.

Junczys-Dowmunt (2019) suggested to use even larger chunks, but that did not seem to work well in our current settings. Already the second model with a maximum of 250 tokens did not converge to any reasonable result when trained from scratch. We tried to address this problem by initialising the larger model with a pre-trained 100-token model but this approach did not lead to satisfactory results either. Therefore, we exclude all models larger than 100 tokens from our discussions below.

All models are based on the standard Transformer architecture and were trained with MarianNMT (Junczys-Dowmunt et al., 2018). For the WMT EN→DE models, we added 10.3M lines of backtranslations. These backtranslations consisted of German news documents (News2018) translated to English with a sentence-level model; document boundaries were kept intact. We did not include backtranslations for the opposite translation direction to investigate their impact on discourse-level translation.

Our experiments with recently proposed hierarchical attention networks for document-level NMT, in particular Miculicich et al. (2018) and Maruf et al. (2019), either underperformed or could not cope with the data sizes and document lengths of our training sets. For comparison, we nevertheless report results of a selective attention (Maruf et al., 2019) model for the WMT

EN→DE task. This model has to be trained in a two-step procedure: (1) a standard sentence-level model is trained on all the training data and, (2) a document-level model is trained on top of the sentence-level model that adds the inter-sentential information from the surrounding context using the attentive connections of the extended network. We focused on source-side attention for the wider context and did not explore further setups due to computational costs and unsatisfactory baseline results. Otherwise, we use the standard settings recommended in the released software.

5 Evaluation

Each system is evaluated on the respective test set using the BLEU (Papineni et al., 2002) and METEOR (Denkowski and Lavie, 2014) metrics. In particular, we evaluate each of them on three variants of the test set:

Consistent context: the context sentences of the test set are appended in their natural order, as they appear in the data.

Inconsistent context: the test set is shuffled such that the context sentences are random.

No context: each sentence of the test set is considered its own document, so no contextual information is made available.

This setup allows us to check whether observed improvements are due to the additional context or to other factors.[10] A good context-aware system should perform best with consistent context and worst with inconsistent context.

Note that the concatenation models need some special treatment at test time. The sliding window approaches need to be post-processed in order to remove non-relevant parts of the translation in all cases where we train models with extended target language content. For simplicity, we rely on the segment separation tokens that are produced in translation similar to the ones seen during training. We have found this approach to be very robust, in the sense that the models reliably learn to place them at appropriate positions.

For the non-sliding window approaches with fixed maximum size, sentence splitting is not as straightforward and requires some additional treatment. Segments are also separated by separation tokens but we realized that they do not necessarily match with the segment boundaries in the reference data even though the original paper suggests that this should be rather stable (Junczys-Dowmunt, 2019). This is especially fatal if the number of segments does not match. Therefore, we apply standard sentence alignment based on length-correlation and lexical matches using hunalign (Varga et al., 2005) to link the system output to the reference translations. The reported results from the fixed-size models are based on this approach.

5.1 Generic translation metrics

We report BLEU and METEOR scores for all our experiments in Tables 4 and 5. The results and significance tests were computed using *MultEval* (Clark et al., 2011).

By and large, the concatenation models are able to exploit contextual information: BLEU as well as METEOR scores decrease by statistically significant amounts if the context is inconsistent or absent. However, it is difficult to distinguish a winning configuration. In particular, the system that obtains the highest absolute scores is not necessarily the one that learns most from contextual information. The *1Prev+Curr → 1Prev+Curr* system obtains the highest absolute scores among sliding window systems in all four tasks, but is not particularly affected by context inconsistencies. On the other hand, the system using target-language data is most perturbed when context is inconsistent or absent, at least for the OST dataset.[11] It seems therefore that target-language context is as least as important as source-language context. Comparative numbers on the WMT dataset are all very similar, making it hard to draw conclusions.

The 100T fixed-window models perform competitively in terms of absolute scores, compared to the sliding window approaches, despite the alignment problems mentioned above.[12] The compar-

[10]For example, the *1Prev + Curr → Curr* system sees each source sentence twice as often as the *Curr → Curr* system, which might affect general model performance without necessarily improving context awareness.

[11]Note however that we feed the reference instead of the system output at test time for efficiency reasons. Therefore, the numbers cannot be directly compared directly with the other systems, which do not have access to this oracle-type information.

[12]Due to realignment, the number of sentences in the test set varies slightly, which prevents us from computing significance scores. Therefore, the absence of the significance marker * on the *100T → 100T* result lines does not mean that

Dataset:	OST EN → DE						WMT EN → DE					
Context:	Consistent		Incons. (Δ)		None (Δ)		Consistent		Incons. (Δ)		None (Δ)	
System	B	M	B	M	B	M	B	M	B	M	B	M
Curr → Curr (baseline)	21.7	42.6	0.0	0.0	0.0	0.0	39.3	56.9	0.0	0.0	0.0	0.0
1Prev+Curr → Curr	20.9	41.6	-0.3*	-0.5*	-0.2	-0.2	37.6	55.3	-0.5*	-0.3*	-0.2	-0.4*
1Prev+Curr+1Next → Curr	20.1	40.8	-1.0*	-1.2*	-0.6*	-0.5*	34.7	52.3	-0.4*	-0.4*	-0.5*	-0.4*
2Prev+Curr → Curr	20.3	40.4	-0.6*	-0.8*	-0.8*	-0.4*	34.9	53.1	-0.3*	-0.3*	-0.4*	-0.4*
1Prev+Curr → 1Prev+Curr	22.5	43.2	-0.7*	-0.7*	-0.3*	-0.5*	**39.6**	**57.3**	-0.5*	-0.4*	-0.2	-0.3*
1Prev+Curr+1Next → 1Prev+Curr	21.5	42.8	-0.5*	-1.0*	-0.1	-0.6*	38.5	56.0	**-0.8***	**-0.6***	-0.6*	-0.6*
1PrevTarget+Curr → Curr	22.0	42.5	-1.4*	-1.5*	**-1.3***	-1.3*	37.7	55.6	-0.4*	-0.3*	**-0.7***	**-0.7***
100T → 100T	**22.9**	**44.4**	**-1.9**	**-1.9**	-0.5	**-1.8**	39.0	57.2	-0.4	-0.5	0.0	**-0.7**
Selective attention	–	–	–	–	–	–	34.8	53.0	0.0	0.0	-0.2	-0.2

Table 4: BLEU (B) and METEOR (M) scores for EN → DE translation. Absolute scores are reported for the Consistent setting, whereas differences (relative to Consistent) are reported for the Inconsistent and None settings. Statistical significance at $p < 0.05$, obtained by bootstrap resampling, is marked with *.

Dataset:	OST DE → EN						WMT DE → EN					
Context:	Consistent		Incons. (Δ)		None (Δ)		Consistent		Incons. (Δ)		None (Δ)	
System	B	M	B	M	B	M	B	M	B	M	B	M
Curr → Curr (baseline)	27.4	27.6	0.0	0.0	0.0	0.0	34.9	**34.9**	0.0	0.0	0.0	0.0
1Prev+Curr → Curr	26.7	26.8	-0.4*	-0.3*	-0.3*	-0.1*	31.6	32.3	-0.3	0.0	-0.8*	-0.5*
1Prev+Curr+1Next → Curr	24.7	25.5	-0.1	-0.1	-0.3*	0.0	23.0	26.5	-0.1	0.0	**-2.2***	-0.3*
2Prev+Curr → Curr	26.0	26.3	-0.7*	-0.3*	-0.6*	-0.1*	22.0	26.1	-0.1	0.0	-1.3*	**-0.8***
1Prev+Curr → 1Prev+Curr	27.5	27.7	-0.3*	-0.2*	-0.4*	-0.2*	**35.0**	**34.9**	**-0.4***	0.0	-0.9*	-0.5*
1Prev+Curr+1Next → 1Prev+Curr	20.7	24.3	-0.1	0.0	+3.3*	+0.6*	31.2	32.4	-0.3*	**-0.2***	-1.5*	-0.6*
1PrevTarget+Curr → Curr	26.9	27.0	-1.0*	-0.7*	-1.0*	-0.6*	32.7	33.2	-0.3	0.0	-1.1*	-0.5*
100T → 100T	**29.3**	**28.8**	**-1.6**	**-1.0**	**-2.2**	**-1.3**	34.7	**34.9**	+0.1	+0.1	-0.7	-0.3

Table 5: BLEU (B) and METEOR (M) scores for DE → EN translation.

	anaphoric								event	pleonastic	
	it				they		it/they		it	it	
	intra		inter		intra	inter	sing.	group			
	subj.	non-subj.	subj.	non-subj.							**Total**
Examples:	*25*	*25*	*25*	*25*	*10*	*10*	*5*	*15*	*30*	*30*	***200***
OST Curr → Curr	9	7	6	7	5	3	1	5	20	28	91
OST 1Prev + Curr → 1Prev + Curr	10	6	12	9	5	6	1	2	24	25	100
WMT Curr → Curr	14	12	9	10	5	4	0	8	20	26	108
WMT 1Prev + Curr → 1Prev + Curr	9	11	13	12	5	5	1	5	19	28	108

Table 6: Absolute numbers of PROTEST EN → DE pronoun translations evaluated semi-automatically as correct.

DE Pronouns:	ich, es, das, wir, sich, Sie, er, du, sie, die, was, mir, mich, uns, der, man, dich, ihn, dir, dies, ihm, ihr, wer, 's, Ihnen, dem, denen, euch, ihnen, den, Ihr, diese, dessen, deren, einen, dieser, wen, welche, einem, wem, dieses, jene, diesen, dasselbe, welches, einander
Ambiguous:	Sie, den, denen, der, die, diese, dieser, ihm, ihn, ihnen, ihr, man, mich, mir, sich, sie, uns
EN Pronouns:	I, you, it, we, he, what, me, they, who, she, him, them, us, her, himself, itself, themselves, one, yourself, myself, whom, ourselves, i, 'em, herself, mine, yours, ya
Ambiguous:	her, him, it, me, myself, one, she, them, they, us, who, whom, you, yourself
EN Connectives:	although, even though, since, though, meanwhile, while, yet, however
DE Negations:	nicht, nie, niemand, nichts, nirgends, nirgendwo, kein, weder
EN Negations:	no, not, never, nobody, noone, no-one, nothing, nowhere, none, neither, nor

Table 7: List of words and lemmas used to detect discourse-level properties.

ison between consistent, inconsistent and absent context reveals a clear difference between the two datasets: For WMT, the results are almost the same for the three scenarios. This can be attributed to the longer sentences in the WMT test set, which makes the 100 token window performing similar to the one without extended context, as discussed in section 4. In contrast, for the subtitle data, we see notable performance drops when disturbing the model with random or absent context. In this dataset, segments are shorter and 100-token windows substantially increase the context that is available for translation (there are 9.68 sentences per chunk on average).

The selective attention model yields absolute scores with consistent context that are not competitive and barely beat the baseline. It also seems to fail to pick up relevant information from the wider document context, as it obtains almost identical results with inconsistent and absent context.

The WMT EN $\rightarrow$ DE models have seen back-translations during training but the DE $\rightarrow$ EN models have not. The results suggest that the additional data helps the models distinguishing consistent from inconsistent input, but further tests will be required to corroborate this hypothesis.

The WMT dataset has shorter documents and longer sentences with more complex discourse-level features. Although this may indicate that it is a more challenging dataset for our models, the performances seem very similar across systems, and it is hard to discriminate informative patterns. However, the inconsistent setting appears to be affected by genre, with none or very small differences with the WMT data, suggesting that the longer sentences are more self-contained in terms of discourse features and that systems effectively pick this signal up. In this same sense (and counterintuitively), the differences between inconsistent and none seem to suggest that as long as the system has access to big enough window, the order in which the document is fed is less important.

5.2 Test suite metrics

Discourse-specific metrics such as Guzmán et al. (2014) would be welcome to assess the translation quality on specific discourse-level features such as those discussed in Section 3.1. However, they have the disadvantage of relying on a discourse parser, which we do not have for German. At least, we are able to evaluate the quality of pronoun translation thanks to the existence of two test suites for English–German pronoun translation: **PROTEST** (Guillou and Hardmeier, 2016; Guillou et al., 2018) is based on TED talks transcripts. These consist of planned speech documents, therefore the genre is somewhere in the middle between news text and dialog. **ContraPro** (Müller et al., 2018) uses material from OpenSubtitles. Due to the overlap of the ContraPro data and our OST training set, we do not use this test suite.

Table 6 reports PROTEST results for two selected systems, the *Curr* $\rightarrow$ *Curr* baseline and the best-performing variable-window concatenation model *1Prev+Curr* $\rightarrow$ *1Prev+Curr*. The results draw on a semi-automatic evaluation scheme, where pronouns are accepted as correct if they match the reference and the remaining pronouns are evaluated by hand. The manual evaluation was done by one of the authors.[13] Overall recall of all systems is around 50%, and the differences between systems are quite small.

It can be seen that the models trained on the news dataset obtain higher recall. This confirms our observation in Section 3.1 that the WMT dataset contains higher numbers of coreference chains and cross-sentence pronominal coreference. The context-aware models show small improvements only in the OST dataset. Crucially, the context-aware models show consistently higher numbers in the category of inter-sentential anaphoric pronouns, one of the categories where the previous sentence context is indeed expected to help most. However, most observed differences may not be statistically significant.

The PROTEST evaluation confirms the findings of the WMT18 evaluation (Guillou et al., 2018). In both of these evaluations the *pleonastic* and *event* categories are the least problematic. *Intra-* and *inter-sentential* pronouns are somewhat in the middle but remain difficult, while cases where the anaphor and the antecedent mismatch in features (*they-singular, it/they group*) are very poorly handled.

6 Conclusion

We have presented two English–German document-level translation datasets and shown that they represent different text genres with

the differences are not significant.

[13]We used the provided tool described in Hardmeier and Guillou (2016).

different distributions of discourse-level features. The context-aware NMT models on these datasets show performance differences that are to some extent indicative of the underlying textual characteristics: the longer sentences in the news dataset make it harder to find differences between training configurations or evaluation setups. Fixed-window approaches show surprisingly good results on the movie subtitles dataset, but the impact of the realignment process remains to be investigated further.

The general performance of a document-level MT system can be assessed by testing translation quality with consistent and artificially scrambled context. Models that are able to learn relevant discourse features will be affected if the context is incoherent or absent. Our results show that this test provides a complementary view on the systems' performances.

Our study further suggests that the connections between discourse features and MT results should be analyzed more thoroughly. The detailed breakdown of the distribution of discourse-level properties could be a first step towards the compilation of property-specific test sets.

Automatic measures can be complemented with manual assessment of the outcome from the different test scenarios, which further reveals the effect of discourse features available to the system. We show that pronoun test suites such as PROTEST are a good start for this assessment, although multilingual coverage remains a problem for a systematic evaluation of this kind.

Acknowledgements

The work in this paper was supported by the FoTran project, funded by the European Research Council (ERC) under the European Union's Horizon 2020 research and innovation programme (grant agreement No 771113), and the MeMAD project, funded by the European Union's Horizon 2020 Research and Innovation Programme under grant agreement No 780069.

The authors wish to acknowledge CSC – IT Center for Science, Finland, for generous computational resources.

References

Ruchit Agrawal, Marco Turchi, and Matteo Negri. 2018. Contextual handling in neural machine translation: Look behind, ahead and on both sides. In *Proceedings of the 21st Annual Conference of the European Association for Machine Translation*, pages 11–20, Alacant, Spain.

Loïc Barrault, Ondřej Bojar, Marta R. Costa-jussá, Christian Federmann, Mark Fishel, Yvette Graham, Barry Haddow, Matthias Huck, Philipp Koehn, Shervin Malmasi, Christof Monz, Mathias Müller, Santanu Pal, Matt Post, and Marcos Zampieri. 2019. Findings of the 2019 Conference on Machine Translation (WMT19). In *Proceedings of the Fourth Conference on Machine Translation*, pages 128–188, Florence, Italy. Association for Computational Linguistics.

Rachel Bawden, Rico Sennrich, Alexandra Birch, and Barry Haddow. 2018. Evaluating discourse phenomena in neural machine translation. In *Proceedings of the 2018 Conference of the North American Chapter of the Association for Computational Linguistics: Human Language Technologies, Volume 1 (Long Papers)*, pages 1304–1313, New Orleans, Louisiana. Association for Computational Linguistics.

Marine Carpuat and Michel Simard. 2012. The trouble with SMT consistency. In *Proceedings of the Seventh Workshop on Statistical Machine Translation*, pages 442–449, Montréal, Canada. Association for Computational Linguistics.

Mauro Cettolo, Girardi Christian, and Federico Marcello. 2012. Wit3: Web inventory of transcribed and translated talks. In *Proceedings of the Conference of the European Association for Machine Translation*, page 261–268.

Jonathan H. Clark, Chris Dyer, Alon Lavie, and Noah A. Smith. 2011. Better hypothesis testing for statistical machine translation: Controlling for optimizer instability. In *Proceedings of the 49th Annual Meeting of the Association for Computational Linguistics: Human Language Technologies*, pages 176–181, Portland, Oregon, USA. Association for Computational Linguistics.

Kevin Clark and Christopher D. Manning. 2016. Deep reinforcement learning for mention-ranking coreference models. In *Empirical Methods on Natural Language Processing*.

Michael Denkowski and Alon Lavie. 2014. Meteor universal: Language specific translation evaluation for any target language. In *Proceedings of the Ninth Workshop on Statistical Machine Translation*, pages 376–380, Baltimore, Maryland, USA. Association for Computational Linguistics.

Federico Fancellu and Bonnie Webber. 2015. Translating negation: Induction, search and model errors. In *Proceedings of the Ninth Workshop on Syntax, Semantics and Structure in Statistical Translation*, pages 21–29, Denver, Colorado, USA. Association for Computational Linguistics.

Zhengxian Gong, Min Zhang, Chewlim Tan, and Guodong Zhou. 2012. N-gram-based tense models for statistical machine translation. In *Proceedings of the 2012 Joint Conference on Empirical Methods in Natural Language Processing and Computational Natural Language Learning*, EMNLP-CoNLL 2012, pages 276–285, Jeju Island, Korea. Association for Computational Linguistics.

Liane Guillou. 2012. Improving pronoun translation for statistical machine translation. In *Proceedings of the Student Research Workshop at the 13th Conference of the European Chapter of the Association for Computational Linguistics*, pages 1–10, Avignon, France. Association for Computational Linguistics.

Liane Guillou and Christian Hardmeier. 2016. Protest: A test suite for evaluating pronouns in machine translation. In *Proceedings of the Tenth International Conference on Language Resources and Evaluation (LREC 2016)*. European Language Resources Association (ELRA).

Liane Guillou, Christian Hardmeier, Ekaterina Lapshinova-Koltunski, and Sharid Loáiciga. 2018. A pronoun test suite evaluation of the English–German MT systems at WMT 2018. In *Proceedings of the Third Conference on Machine Translation: Shared Task Papers*, pages 570–577, Belgium, Brussels. Association for Computational Linguistics.

Francisco Guzmán, Shafiq Joty, Lluís Màrquez, and Preslav Nakov. 2014. Using discourse structure improves machine translation evaluation. In *Proceedings of the 52nd Annual Meeting of the Association for Computational Linguistics*, pages 687–698, Baltimore, Maryland. Association for Computational Linguistics.

Najeh Hajlaoui and Andrei Popescu-Belis. 2013. Assessing the accuracy of discourse connective translations: Validation of an automatic metric. In *Proceedings of the 14th International Conference on Intelligent Text Processing and Computational Linguistics*, University of the Aegean, Samos, Greece.

Christian Hardmeier and Marcello Federico. 2010. Modelling pronominal anaphora in statistical machine translation. In *Proceedings of the 7th International Workshop on Spoken Language Translation*, IWSLT 2010, pages 283–289, Paris, France.

Christian Hardmeier and Liane Guillou. 2016. A graphical pronoun analysis tool for the PROTEST pronoun evaluation test suite. In *Proceedings of the 19th Annual Conference of the European Association for Machine Translation*, pages 318–330.

Christian Hardmeier, Jörg Tiedemann, and Joakim Nivre. 2013. Latent anaphora resolution for cross-lingual pronoun prediction. In *Proceedings of the 2013 Conference on Empirical Methods in Natural Language Processing*, pages 380–391, Seattle, Washington, USA. Association for Computational Linguistics.

Sebastien Jean, Stanislas Lauly, Orhan Firat, and Kyunghyun Cho. 2017. Does neural machine translation benefit from larger context? In *arXiv preprint, arXiv:1704.05135*.

Marcin Junczys-Dowmunt. 2019. Microsoft Translator at WMT 2019: Towards large-scale document-level neural machine translation. In *Proceedings of the Fourth Conference on Machine Translation*, pages 424–432, Florence, Italy. Association for Computational Linguistics.

Marcin Junczys-Dowmunt, Roman Grundkiewicz, Tomasz Dwojak, Hieu Hoang, Kenneth Heafield, Tom Neckermann, Frank Seide, Ulrich Germann, Alham Fikri Aji, Nikolay Bogoychev, André F. T. Martins, and Alexandra Birch. 2018. Marian: Fast neural machine translation in C++. In *Proceedings of ACL 2018, System Demonstrations*, pages 116–121, Melbourne, Australia. Association for Computational Linguistics.

Ekaterina Lapshinova-Koltunski and Christian Hardmeier. 2017. Discovery of discourse-related language contrasts through alignment discrepancies in English-German translation. In *Proceedings of the Third Workshop on Discourse in Machine Translation*, pages 73–81, Copenhagen, Denmark. Association for Computational Linguistics.

Ekaterina Lapshinova-Koltunski, Sharid Loáiciga, Christian Hardmeier, and Pauline Krielke. 2019. Cross-lingual incongruences in the annotation of coreference. In *Proceedings of the Second Workshop on Computational Models of Reference, Anaphora and Coreference*, pages 26–34, Minneapolis, USA. Association for Computational Linguistics.

Pierre Lison and Jörg Tiedemann. 2016. OpenSubtitles2016: Extracting large parallel corpora from movie and TV subtitles. In *Proceedings of the Tenth International Conference on Language Resources and Evaluation (LREC 2016)*, Paris, France. European Language Resources Association (ELRA).

Sharid Loáiciga, Thomas Meyer, and Andrei Popescu-Belis. 2014. English-French verb phrase alignment in Europarl for tense translation modeling. In *Proceedings of the Ninth International Conference on Language Resources and Evaluation (LREC'14)*. European Language Resources Association (ELRA).

Christopher D. Manning, Mihai Surdeanu, John Bauer, Jenny Finkel, Steven J. Bethard, and David McClosky. 2014. The Stanford CoreNLP natural language processing toolkit. In *Association for Computational Linguistics (ACL) System Demonstrations*, pages 55–60.

Sameen Maruf, André F. T. Martins, and Gholamreza Haffari. 2019. Selective attention for context-aware neural machine translation. In *Proceedings of the 2019 Conference of the North American Chapter of the Association for Computational Linguistics: Human Language Technologies, Volume 1 (Long and Short Papers)*, pages 3092–3102, Minneapolis, Minnesota. Association for Computational Linguistics.

Thomas Meyer and Andrei Popescu-Belis. 2012. Using sense-labeled discourse connectives for statistical machine translation. In *Proceedings of the Workshop on Hybrid Approaches to Machine Translation at EACL 2012*, HyTra, pages 129—138, Avignon, France.

Thomas Meyer, Andrei Popescu-Belis, Najeh Hajlaoui, and Andrea Gesmundo. 2012. Machine translation of labeled discourse connectives. In *Proceedings of the Tenth Biennial Conference of the Association for Machine Translation in the Americas*, AMTA 2012.

Lesly Miculicich, Dhananjay Ram, Nikolaos Pappas, and James Henderson. 2018. Document-level neural machine translation with hierarchical attention networks. In *Proceedings of the 2018 Conference on Empirical Methods in Natural Language Processing*, pages 2947–2954, Brussels, Belgium. Association for Computational Linguistics.

Mathias Müller, Annette Rios, Elena Voita, and Rico Sennrich. 2018. A large-scale test set for the evaluation of context-aware pronoun translation in neural machine translation. In *Proceedings of the Third Conference on Machine Translation: Research Papers*, pages 61–72, Belgium, Brussels. Association for Computational Linguistics.

Robert Östling and Jörg Tiedemann. 2016. Efficient word alignment with Markov Chain Monte Carlo. *Prague Bulletin of Mathematical Linguistics*, 106:125–146.

Kishore Papineni, Salim Roukos, Todd Ward, and Wei-Jing Zhu. 2002. Bleu: a method for automatic evaluation of machine translation. In *Proceedings of the 40th Annual Meeting of the Association for Computational Linguistics*, pages 311–318, Philadelphia, Pennsylvania, USA. Association for Computational Linguistics.

Andrei Popescu-Belis. 2019. Context in neural machine translation: A review of models and evaluations.

Anita Ramm and Alexander Fraser. 2016. Modeling verbal inflection for English to German SMT. In *Proceedings of the First Conference on Machine Translation: Volume 1, Research Papers*, pages 21–31, Berlin, Germany. Association for Computational Linguistics.

Annette Rios, Mathias Müller, and Rico Sennrich. 2018. The word sense disambiguation test suite at WMT18. In *Proceedings of the Third Conference on Machine Translation: Shared Task Papers*, pages 588–596, Belgium, Brussels. Association for Computational Linguistics.

Annette Rios Gonzales, Laura Mascarell, and Rico Sennrich. 2017. Improving word sense disambiguation in neural machine translation with sense embeddings. In *Proceedings of the Second Conference on Machine Translation*, pages 11–19, Copenhagen, Denmark. Association for Computational Linguistics.

Rico Sennrich, Barry Haddow, and Alexandra Birch. 2016. Controlling politeness in neural machine translation via side constraints. In *Proceedings of the 2016 Conference of the North American Chapter of the Association for Computational Linguistics: Human Language Technologies*, pages 35–40, San Diego, California. Association for Computational Linguistics.

Karin Sim Smith. 2017. On integrating discourse in machine translation. In *Proceedings of the Third Workshop on Discourse in Machine Translation*, pages 110–121, Copenhagen, Denmark. Association for Computational Linguistics.

Jörg Tiedemann and Yves Scherrer. 2017. Neural machine translation with extended context. In *Proceedings of the Third Workshop on Discourse in Machine Translation*, pages 82–92, Copenhagen, Denmark. Association for Computational Linguistics.

Don Tuggener. 2016. *Incremental coreference resolution for German*. Ph.D. thesis, University of Zürich.

Daniel Varga, Péter Halácsy, András Kornai, Viktor Nagy, László Németh, and Viktor Trón. 2005. Parallel corpora for medium density languages. In *Proceedings of RANLP 2005*, pages 590–596.

Elena Voita, Rico Sennrich, and Ivan Titov. 2019. When a good translation is wrong in context: Context-aware machine translation improves on deixis, ellipsis, and lexical cohesion. In *Proceedings of the 57th Annual Meeting of the Association for Computational Linguistics*, pages 1198–1212, Florence, Italy. Association for Computational Linguistics.

Elena Voita, Pavel Serdyukov, Rico Sennrich, and Ivan Titov. 2018. Context-aware neural machine translation learns anaphora resolution. In *Proceedings of the 56th Annual Meeting of the Association for Computational Linguistics (Volume 1: Long Papers)*, pages 1264–1274, Melbourne, Australia. Association for Computational Linguistics.

Author Index

Creus, Carles, 13

España-Bonet, Cristina, 1, 13

Kamigaito, Hidetaka, 45
Kim, Yunsu, 24

Lapshinova-Koltunski, Ekaterina, 1
Loáiciga, Sharid, 51

Martínez Garcia, Eva, 13

Nagata, Masaaki, 45
Ney, Hermann, 24

Ohtani, Takumi, 45
Okumura, Manabu, 45

Scherrer, Yves, 51
Sugiyama, Amane, 35

Tiedemann, Jörg, 51
Tran, Duc Thanh, 24

van Genabith, Josef, 1

Yoshinaga, Naoki, 35

Association for Computational Linguistics
209 N. Eighth Street
Stroudsburg, Pennsylvania 18360

ISBN 978-1-7138-0079-8

9 781713 800798

CURRAN ASSOCIATES INC.
proceedings.com

Third Workshop on Multilingual Surface Realisation (MSR 2020)

Held online due to COVID-19

Barcelona, Spain
12 December 2020